SELECTIVE STIMULUS

by

Stanton Kelley

FIRST EDITION

Copyright 1998, by Stanton Kelley
Library of Congress Catalog Card No: 97-90770
ISBN: 1-56002-768-1

UNIVERSITY EDITIONS, Inc.
59 Oak Lane, Spring Valley
Huntington, West Virginia 25704

Cover by Brendon and Brian Fraim

Dedication

**For
Posterity**

**For
The Enlightened**

*For
Marianne, Ted,
Betty and Bob,
Vincent, Keith, and Eddy.*

ACKNOWLEDGEMENTS

This compulsive literary work owes its birth to the collective labor of: My mother, Betty, Sylvie Targhetta, Keith Carlton Kelley, and Rabbi Allen Freehling.

A special thanks to Marianne Uhe, the project's ever present midwife.

TABLE OF CONTENTS

THE VOICE

Please do not disturb . . .

Seems nowadays a request absurd.

Longing search for inner voice

Gone unheard . . .

On the verge of . . .

Answered.

THE JOURNEY

A cluster of freshly liberated leaves
Soar swiftly from the confines
Of autumn's yellow-red canopy,

To a joyous ride astride a fast-moving
Sun-splashed stream . . .
A roller-cascade release afloat a gushing waterway.

While a myriad of anticipant vegetation await their turn.
Dislodged twigs . . . excited by a journey rejuvenation,
Whole branches snapped in the wind . . .
Find the navigation an exhilarating challenge.

All of nature's bounty . . . happy to find themselves
Where they are presently—
Amid the refreshing stimulus of wanderlust!

Butterflies, nymphs and crickets glide side by side
Or hitch a ride, on the backs of foliage felicitous.

All, are the hasten-fallen—
One step closer to oblivion.

Taken with the inspirational transition . . .
A new juxtaposition . . .
Appreciation driven.

A THOUSAND STEEDS

A thousand steeds came thundering . . .
Racing in a dust dream—hoof pounding
Sweating, head bobbing, nose flaring.
Advancing . . .

Shaking Earth's foundation
Rattling Mother's crusty core.

Suddenly, the massive equine were upon me—a stampede!
I stood my ground, as the exquisite muscle-mass passed;

The force of their vital energy
Transferred into the fiber of my being—
Power harnessed . . . prowess enhanced

Organs oxygenated . . . elongated, inflated!

Exhilarated to the extreme,
I awoke from this equestrian dream,
Embraced my lady lying next to me—
Passionately possessed . . . fervor famished—in need of express.

Bodies finding subliminal release in spent lust,
Found ourselves curiously blanketed
In a bed or red earthen dust.

RENEWAL

Dawn slips into consciousness
And the levels of life's existences make themselves evident . . .

Dark obliterate—non-apparent forms materialize . . .
Arrive like new previously non-existent entities—
Hastily shaped and cast to the forefront of cognizance.

Molecular structures whose myriad particles
Miraculously synthesize into tangible reality.

To this, a compliment of stereophonic accents . . .
A dimensionally-deep, audio menagerie experience—
Of full sensory enhancement, poised for presentment
With golden sliver solar debut; from black obscurity,
To gilded radiance deliverance anew.

TOSCANA

Tuscany, there is no other beauty can match thee.

Set my eyes upon your serene valleys . . .

To meander down the color-splash embroidery

Of red poppy flowered meadows that enchant

The antiquitus vestments of your hilltop cities.

Grant me taste of your spirit, exalted cuisine,

And favor of cathedral bells ring.

Oh charming Tuscany, ever so praise worthy:

Earthen, stalwart, spell-binding special place . . .

To you my heart is tethered in perpetual embrace.

RECOGNIZED EYES

Weaned on cornbread and collard greens,
To toil in the hot cotton fields
Of a buttermilk sky.

Sweat-soaked, yoked to the land,
Crop-share stained of pricked bleeding hands.

Day is done,
Dream of maws, yams and chitterlings . . .
But, a recurring vision disturbs the evening peace—
Nightmarish!

Mind locked, forced to stare face to face
With an overworked, old and graying black mule.
Uncanny, is the resemblance to
Uncle John and aunt Jewel.

Invariably, the mule image would fade—then rise.
With it, went the dead-eye suffering
Of a fellow recognized.

BLACK FACE

Spoke with Aunt Jamima today . . .
Got an earful of what she had to say.
Her bulk-black exploited, mis-conceptualized
Stereotypical Negroid face,
Twitching in anguished recall of commercial debase.

"Just awful" she said,
As she lowered her large bigot-reduced head.
Words . . . thought evocative of injury—
Succinct, heart wrenching;

Born of time inflicted abuse—
Obtuse misuse . . .
A nation's pictured indignity . . .
Portrait hung in effigy,
An entire Race . . .
The victim of commercial disgrace.

WHITE BIRD

WHITE BIRD you are so happy to be white.

Perhaps you deserve to coo.

White is pure,
White is clean,
White is good,
White is right.

Naturally, you are entitled to the accolades—

It is your birth right.

But, what are you to make of black?

Pure black is the absence of color—

No birth right?

WHITE BIRD,

Look to the peacock

Who is Multicolor and proud!

OLD GLORY

I observed Old Glory
Wind tattered, but still flowing;

A pictorial commentary
On a nation's *inhabitants condition.*

In disrepair—but still there,
Subjects subjugated
By the currents of a capricious wind—
Government driven.

SEDUCTIVE EARTH

Like a woman quietly slipping into her negligee,
With silent stealth did the night slip into day.
Lush-wet was the lingering residue of mist
Not yet sun kissed.
Earth's hot steam rose to rise in liberation
Up to the sky.

And—

Diffused light played upon droplets atop emerald blades of grass;
Giving splash and sparkle of a diamond encrusted crown.
Inebriated with nature's intoxicants,
I threw myself upon the ground.

Lustfully my body sought to soak up Her Majesty.
I rolled around—all over her wet pubis of grass and mulch
My loins delightfully found.
With abandoned joy did I explore . . .
A co-mingle of juice galore.

I lay exhausted, smiling with pleasure for having played
This private fantasy game—
And just realized that I "came."

SAN FRANCISCO

A silver bird lifted me high into the sky.

Sunlit and aglow, the East Bay below filled my window.

But, where was San Francisco? Where on earth did it go?

Eerie and surreal was this absence of concrete and steel.

No form-no feature, as though an avalanche

of snow had swallowed up cable cars, homes,

steeples and all the city's people.

A metallic amphibian-like creature stretched its groping

Tentacles into a dense fluff of cumulus;

While pairs of luminous eyes sped across its back

And vanished into a milk-white nimbus.

The jumbo bird banked its wings, and there!

Just beyond its tip, emerged a sunset-lit Golden Gate!

Put me in euphoric state.

Bridge to my relief, sanguine spance renown,

No more landmark need be found.

A ROSE

Fragrant circular beauty of soft floral essence . . .

Regal and demure—

The height of horticulture.

Blossom of respect, Your gift you protect

With thorn you project.

So pleasing you are to the eye,

A bouquet for his queen,

A king duth buy thee—

Rivals color of a ruby.

Ah, to see, to smell, to touch a rose . . .

To all my senses

Your grandeur I am elatedly exposed.

FLOWERS

A cut flower
Plucked from nutrients
Is rapidly aging . . .
Deteriorating from deprivation
Sacrificed by insensitive, life-obtuse behavior.

A rooted flower flourishes
In life sustaining element . . .
Soiled, but unspoiled
By interruptive hands . . .
It stands and grows—
Removed from the throws
Of premature whither and death.

The floret placed side by side . . .
Though of some semblance,
Soon have no common resemblance.

LETTING GO

Acts of generosity
Complete a full-circle energy flow.

To begrudgingly bestow,
Constricts the flow to an arduous letting go.

And . . .

When opportunity to share
Is viewed as dreaded obligation,
The flow shuts down,
To the frown
Of constipation.

D E V I A T E S

Gingerly, he ventured
Into another world.
One that spoke softly
But, dogmatically of pseudo-civility.

Where conformity supersedes substance,
And pretense is essence.

Where illusion is standard,
And delusion is premium.

Confused, he sought solace . . .
Found it in a fellow misfit.

With syncopated acknowledgment,
There was swift/mutual abandonment.

Only a trace of static cellophane remained,
On the deviates it had temporarily claimed.

EXCHANGE

How truly wonderful is the engagement

Of the mind of an intellect . . .

A singularly sparce experience,

Magnanimous by virtue of its rarity.

A smattering of insanity I detect . . .

Sprinkled with a generous enrapture of genius.

This, the powerful sea-flow of aphrodisia

Rushed into the tide pools of my brain,

To recede in delightful recall indelible.

YARDSTICK

And what pray tell
Is the measure of a man . . .
The number of pretty *birds* held in hand?
Many is less than one . . .
For with crowd, their song is gone.

Or, perhaps it's financial position?
That platform is only as sturdy
As is the attendant mental condition.

Some would argue for lingual eloquence.
Absent of sincerity, the proposition
Has neither validity nor relevance.

The *true* measure of a man . . .
A calibrated rule devised of elemental integrity,
A rise to its apex is the greatest ascent
Of human development.

Absent this rudimentary essential,
The other components
Are inconsequential.

Apparition

Suffocated in sizzling sand,
rests the ravished carcass
Of a desert town succumb
To the bite of a zillion silica particles.

Sun bleached, splintered rooftops
Ride the crest of a white-hot powdered sea . . .

And a semi-liberated door frame
Raps and taps . . . hauntingly,
In disjointed syncopated reply
To a hinged sign post's
Dry, parch-throated cry.

Gust of wind reveals
A whispered conversation
Concealed under the scorched planks,
Of the wooden sidewalk around back.

Sunset . . .
Saloon sounds of whiskey shot glasses smashed down.
Another round . . . a drunken brawl confounds . . .
Result of a lady's virtue, victim found.

Just now,
A lone Indian strides into this entombed homestead;
His bearing and presence too proud to be among the dead.
With purposeful focus, this non-ghost
Trudged through drifts of sand—
Among the populous hosts of ghosts,
Up to a hitching post.

Reaching out into thin air . . .
A magnificent pony was instantaneously there!
Seemed to appear from nowhere.

With one swift motion,
The Brave mounted the Paint
And cantered toward a cliff side encampment.

From his hilltop abode,
The Indigenous stranger observed the descent
Of a brilliant ball-fire glow . . .
Creation of a panorama indigo.

The execution . . .
A final swallow
Of a ghost infested hallow
That once lay sprawled below.

BLANCO

Everywhere the eye could see there were bodies . . .
Surrounded by them—succumb to them.
Brown, round, beautiful bodies . . . feminine
With succulent, translucent skins.

Sultry . . . of maternity . . . erotic—evocative,
They lay dormant; imploring eyes wanting me,
Awaiting the snap of my fingers—
Or some other singular signal, to transcend their repose .
To breathe breath—to heave palpitating breasts;
Share completely, their sensuality,
To surrender luscious forlorn loins . . .
Beyond acrylics hung in suspense,
Just beyond inanimate . . .
Just beyond.

CLOSED

He lies terminal on his back—
Down and dying . . .
Succumb to life-long condition.

FEAR, is the worse of his wounds . . .
An open sore,
Festered with marauding maggots
Oozing puss distrust—
Hatred has him gangrene;
And nothing—
No antiviral
No antigen
No antidote
Penetrates this antisocial, antisemetic
ANTI-BODY.
Destined to be eaten from within,
No salve able to soothe or save him.

Faint from the sick odor of self-rot,
Stubbornly, steadfastly, ignorantly
He rejects all dissimilar, healthy influences.

A Black nurse smiles tenderly and strokes his forehead,
And his eyes close to darkness.

CHOCOLATE DREAM

Increasingly,
Every wakeful dream
Is color-splashed
With images of your
Chocolate cream . . . dripping.

Two scoops coned quickly please . . .
Hot tongue in proximity-
Outstretched . . . anticipatory,

To catch a droplet of cocoa sculpt . . .
Your svelte torso melt,
Mussed over my face-
Like a child smeared with
Sticky-rich total membrane taste exchange.

A savored lap of luscious liquid flavor-
Never full-up . . . ever ravenous.

So, surrender you must;
To this fervent lust,
Or waste to a spent, formless lactose puddle
Gone untasted . . . unconsummated.

CANON FODDER

Canon Fodder found, what befell thee?

A nine-millimeter round?

You cannot speak . . .

But, a provision precedes your condition . . .

Next to that spent round of ammunition,

A semblance of some recognition—

A chain linking you to your . . .

DOG TAG.

REALITY CHECK

Lost to a stuporous suspension in cyberspace . . .
I am marveled, mesmerized, and manipulated;
By an electronic Icon
That is as indifferent to me as a dead friend.

Enslaved . . . shackled and locked away
In the deep dark dungeon of self indulgence—
Prisoner to the computer.

A strange force has me in a strangle-hold
That grips my throat and presses my head
Attentively forward—
Affixed to a screen amuck with moronic logicians.

Drunk am I on these brain saturate intoxicants . . .
Leaving me with a colossal hangover,
And an insatiable craving for more.

The elixir has begun to exact its toll . . .
Red aching eye balls hang disjointedly from their sockets . . .
Zapped by untold volumes of yet-to-be identified radiants.

It is a strange sort of stimulated simulation;
Beckoning me to crawl inside its tube
And cavort with an artificial intelligentsia.

I fear that I have become . . . a refugee from the real—
Out of touch, and fornicator with virtual reality.

PRAYER FOR NATURE

Crisp mountain air invigorates my spirit.

The soothing sound of rocks

Kissed by a meandering stream . . .

Oh, how I long to hear it.

This . . . the everlasting . . . the real—

The stuff upon which our souls heal.

Give me more . . . a glut, I can not get enough.

Set your forest aglow in mid-day sun . . .

Bring on a canopy of stars when day is done.

Let me live it a thousand fold;

For there be no more beautiful fairytale told.

ODE TO THE OCEAN

Deep cavernous body of ominous mood and capricious spirit,

Crash and thrash your coiled mass of froth and energy.

Pound and pulverize what you will.

-THEN LAY STILL-

GENTLY . . .

Return me to familiar womb left long ago . . .

In rhythmic tempo of your ebb and flow.

Slip silently in and out my mind's window.

Sleep, while the stars and moon shimmer

With brilliance upon your repose.

Day and night, come back again and again—

Like the kept promise of a faithful friend.

Free-willed marvel of the universe . . .

Cantankerous, captivating, perverse.

Smooth and polish your rocks, carve your cliffs,

Let wind-filled sails play, and feed your children every day.

—Would have you no other way—

SURF

Speak to me

Frothy surf pounding shore,

Recede to whisper . . .

Then return in uproar.

Boast of your explore,

With splash and pour of mirth and muse—

Or devastation, if you so choose.

A baited fish you have curious.

Idle and rapturous at coastline . . .

Awaiting hook of your story line.

SEA CRY

The ocean is inordinately audible today . . .
Swells pounding the sand—seeking attention.
She spoke to me, waves breaking into soliloquy;
A splattering account of her dominion's
Inhabitants current condition.

A ledger-like inventory was given,
Triumphs and tragedies
Delivered in measured voice—
Steady and unshaken;

The negative outdistancing the positive
By an immense-largely anticipated margin:

Porpoise population on the mend . . .
Humpback Whale's missed presence . . .
Manatee's sad demise . . .
Abalone principally gone for eternity.

Such was her litany.
Somewhere near the end of this soliloquies plead,
She emitted a wrenching sibilant sigh—

Made me want to cry.
I walked on . . .
Waved goodbye.

I'M HOME

I know I'm home . . .
When Bullfrogs and crickets
Get to whoop'n it up—

Give credit to the ole Hoot Owl
For my sleep disrupt.

The Catfish are fat and feisty—
So too are the Wiley Crappie.

My Grandpa and I share a sip
from a bottle of moonshine whiskey,
And a walk together through the lake shore's tall grass,
Is Cotton Mouth risky.

The stars are as big as shiny-new hub caps,
And midday sun is cue to take a nap.

Yes, I know I'm home.

Little Secrets

It was a sweltering Carolina night . . .
The moon shone shiny bright,
Light'n Bugs alight.

Tess and I sit'n on the front porch half undressed.
Guess these hot eve'nins we curse—
But secretly it's the reverse—one's we love best.

We slow down,
Wait for a breeze,

Tess looks at my sweat'n chest,
And I'm a love'n her beautiful wet breasts!

ROCK'N

An old one bedroom shack
Leans in the outback.
A busted plank creaks
When the ole Black Man
Rocks his chair to the rhythm
Of the wind a-blow'n,
The rooster a-crow'n,
Sweet serenity a-flow'n.
All, melodiously-mixed with sultry sound
Of his grandson and wife remember'n
The birds and the bees.

NATURE'S WILL

A fierce wind caught me . . .
Feared I'd be swept out to sea—
Amongst the Anemone.

Decided to relax . . . stay loose . . . let nature's will
Do what she wished with me.

Instantly whisked away was I,
Up into the turbulent sky.

Lite as a kite I flew,
Skimming crests of wild white caped curled fury.

A powerful burst of wind sent me soaring . . .
Up-drafted, to zip high into the sky;
Then, return again . . . vortex fallen.

A second gust, put an end to this respite.
My body thrust at reckless speed
Hurling me uncontrollably over the tumultuous deep.

Just below the ocean's surface,
I could see a school of Dolphin—and they me.

We raced up and down the coast—
Then, far off into the horizon.
Amazing, the sea creatures could keep up with my velocity.
Alternately, tiring and exhilarating fun—
Emotional and spirit gamut run.

Suddenly,
Like a ruptured balloon,
The bottom fell out of my sail.

I came crashing down—
Dumped unceremoniously into Neptune's frigid menagerie.

Surely, this spelled the end for me.
Barely had I digested the severity of my fate . . .
Than appeared my playmates!

The mammals formed a circle, and gently mouthed me;
Then, converged under my belly,
Lifting me out of the sea—
Upon their backs I rode gleefully.
Exhausted, I lay prone—panting.

I relaxed, and let nature do what she would with me.

Presently,
I found myself beached upon the shore.
Hordes gathered around,
Gawking and listening to tooth shiver-chatter sound.

A kind and thoughtful individual threw a blanket down.
As she knelt to tuck me in, much to her chagrin—
A thousand tiny teeth depressions,
And severe burn suffered skin.

Consciousness fading, I overheard a voice asking:
How on earth could anyone fall victim to this condition?

I relaxed, and let nature do what she would with me.

B L U E

Blue . . .
I'm on my way to frolic with you . . .
To immerse in lake, sky, and sea imbue.

To breathe, drink and ingest Blue . . .
Soothing, sensual, satiable hue.

Placate, pacify, pamper me
In soft pastel.

Excite, invite, entreat me—
Dramatically, with deep indigo throw.

Splash Earth's canvass veneer
With wondrous collage-montage.
Found deep in the depths
Of your tincture—far beyond Earth's surface,
Amid Mother's mid-crust;

Color elements miraculous!
Sapphire, Lapis lazuli, and Aquamarine . . .
Precious stones formed in crystalline homage to your tone.

Blue . . .

Love you, now and fully;
For you are of eternity,
And I, of mortality—

Completed surrendered embrace . . .
Knowing that one day,
My body will co-mingle at rest
With your bejeweled earthly elements;
My soul to soar . . . in your azure heaven.

PRIORITIES REGRESSED

Despicable is the devalue
   Of Values . . .
A disgrace of priorities displaced.

Embraced insignificance—
This wallow in the trivial . . .
Mire of sludge ideas recycled;

The money motivated marketplace
Of creative debase.
Subjugated societies of entertained inebriates,
Soak-saturated in Hollywood's
Regurgitated greed . . .
Superstar actors and athletes—
Court jesters . . . crowned Kings.

Wholesale wickedness . . . manifest
Obsessed ill-focus
With the unnatural carnal fixate;
Suffer Sodom and Gomorrah fate
Or fatality . . .
As passively we accept Social Sodomy.

ASTRAL JOURNEY

Awakened was I
By the rumble of muted drums in the distant night.

Advancing.

A pounding of mallets upon taut skins—
Mind-flesh and stick enmeshed.

Pulsating.

The heavy thud of percussion
Sends quarters reeling in concave and convex convulsions.

Suddenly,
The flickering light of a thousand torches
Burst my abode into flames . . .

Walls and ceiling cloaked with
Silhouette of ancestor's risen from the grave.

The apparitions seemed to be
Personas non-threatening—
Wrapped-up in revel of release.

With this perception,
I relaxed, closed my eyes and commenced
To Astral Ride . . .

Floating in free-willed frolic
Of deceased relatives and relationships—
A mega-gathering,
Everyone communicating excitedly . . .
Found me observing—detached . . . distantly.

Try as I might to interact—
Exact merriment . . . it was useless.
I was invisible!

Trapped between planes of
Space and time . . . the immutable-
Dead of the inscrutable.

MORTALITY

Life's brevity has become clear for me to see . . .

A generation of considerable substance fast becoming a non-entity.

Celebrities elapsed the point of prime . . .

Paled shadows of youthful images once ingrained in mind.

The reputed great, and the renown . . .

An easy chair in arduous retirement they have found.

And upon their worn faces each wears his epitaph.

Many written with mirth, others time besmirched.

And so too, a disclosure awaits for others to read in me;

For there be no mortality escapee.

And in the waning years, a certain fear is common among peers:

Body and soul seeking desperate last quest for eternity,

In a continuum struggle to evade an inexorable slide

Into the unknown venture of a seemingly would-be finality.

LETTING GO

Each is the center of his universe,

And nothing exceeds this universal truth.

Lamentable would be this self-centric reality,

Were it not based—understandably,

In a fear of mortality.

No one dare find fault with the narcissist

Obsessed with the longevity of his breath;

Or with the terminal bed-ridden's

Desperate cling to consciousness.

Hell's demons pursue and possess.

A heavy soul lacks peace—

They will not let rest.

Brimstone and fire . . . the burning of a billion tormented.

And above, float a few sharing entities,

Feather-light, in the bright spance of eternity.

PITY

She is old and wilted;
Never a student of her youth.

And therein lies the pity.

She is a transparently selfish,
Disingenuous, geriatric grovel in greed.
Constituted for deception, in order to receive.

And therein lies the pity.

Attention seeking . . . incessant speaking—
A child given to tantrum roll on the floor,
Forever in need to extract more.

And therein lies the pity.

Ever lonely . . . begs the exhausted tolerant,
For time extended company.

And therein lies the pity.

Unaware of the litany of shortfall,
She will be called into oblivion—
As are we all.
And, beyond doubt,
Count herself among the wonderful,
Loving mortal human beings.

And there, in her grave . . . lies the pity.

OLD SHALLOW

Pained dread, to see the aged walking dead,
Dressed from toe to head in the very finest of threads.

Distressed, not for what the clothing had to say—
No, the contrary . . .

Sad, for what these clothes horses
Never were themselves able to convey.

REVELATION

A lengthy walk through life has uncovered something quite
Revealing . . .
The degree to which insanity is companion to everybody.
Turn a corner here . . . cross the street there—
The marginal-sane and functionally insane . . . everywhere.

Only the inane lay claim to an impeccable state of mind . . .
And these poor fools are not difficult to find.
With rare exception,
The degree of debility is all that deliniates the separation.

A few upright healthy souls can be found.
But, many affect a deceptive civility
To mask the mental deficiencies that abound.

One has little choice but to attend the carnival.
Beset with its myriad observed on the fringe . . .
Those given to listen and converse
With an inaudible whisper,
That redials their brain,
Like an obscene phone call.

Intriguing is this mix of social deviates . . .
The paranoid, the manic-depressive, and the schizophrenic,
All attendants of life's illusion,
All either totally or partially . . . civil deluded—
Myself included.

RESOLVE

Blizzard-blown ice bites our abode's window . . .
With an incessant, crackling drive to burst inside;
While two sets of anxious lungs expel cold claustrophobic breath—
The murderous intruder's invasion
And mockery of mannered mirth.

They are lovers imprisoned in an opaque cell . . .
On verge of burial deep in crystalline Hell.
The merciless onslaught has extinguished
All physical craving—
Sexual passion . . .
Limp and fading.

Higher and higher grow the drifts . . .
Wane and slide of spirits.
An eerie quiet pervades the room.

Frozen in frigid embrace,
He looked upon an unrecognizable face . . .
Eyes resigned and entombed
Imploring his to follow,
Down the dark corridor
Of a white vacuum
Devoid of the resolve to continue.

BLACK MALIGN

I am black . . . but not smut.
Feel the differentiation,
Deep within my colored aching guts.
Black . . . the orchestrated equivalent to evil
And murk of distrust.
Neoclassic literature
Is rife with this despicable stuff.

Not unexpectedly,
The antithesis of black
Is awash in a whitewash of sanctimonious piety.
Pity, opposition to indifference
Exists to such an extent.

Black is the charred butt,
Spewing the diarrhea of a prejudiced societal condition.
Alas, for purpose of contrast,
Someone or something
Must be made to look the ass.

Throughout the ages of time,
Black has been unfairly maligned.
But, in the forefront of consciousness
The perceived black demon
So thoroughly entrenched in mind,
May, in its detractors, a day of reckoning find.

SLAVERY

The mega-crazed contemplate
Soiled hands held up to the
Scrutiny of light . . .

The finding of fingernail filth . . .
The shock and stain indelible . . .
The blood-dip of Black-limbed *Objects* . . .
The dried encrustation of horrific deeds.

A cultured multitude,
Ripped from their roots
Of green jungle terra firma,
By greenback greed.
Massive tufts of *Objects* hacked and scooped from their land,
To be transplanted in inhospitable environs.

Crossbred to produce hybrids . . .
Families separated by
Fear of the injured united . . .
Whipped from cohesion . . .
Beaten into submission.

A thousand rifles thunder . . .
African psyche torn asunder.

The sensitive-crazed recoil from the obscenity!

After 100 years,
Mandela smiles
With the promise of civility.

GENETIC ROLES

She is nine and he is four.

He is a baby, and she is a young lady.

Like a mother, over her brother

She will fuss and muss-up fastidious.

Zip baby's jacket and adjust his cap . . .

They are fledglings genetically enwrapped—

Subjects of personal gender gap.

It's good intentioned sibling benevolence,

With sexual role behavioral relevance.

She, essentially the nurturer,

And he, the reluctant/willing recipient.

A scenario we all come to know . . .

Gender-based, experience exposed.

EXPOSURE

A small yellow ball sat haplessly collecting dust.

A whirlwind caught the stagnate sphere

And cast it from its shelved restraint,

Up into the bright blue sky.

Free

It bounced buoyant over new hills

And rolled through distant valleys;

Accumulating a rich encrustation

Of diverse sand and tactile gravel.

Once diminutive . . .

Now, grown to grand proportions.

Heavy with substance,

No longer victim to a capricious wind.

The sphere returned to the familiar,

Aglow with a coat of character.

REFLECTION

I sat on a mountain peak at 10,000 feet,

And pondered the antics of the city's people

All that distance below.

Poor wretched aggressors,

Fighting for food and hollow—

Some for their very existence.

While just now, my eyes caught the flight

Of an eagle in the distance.

There *is* a better way to live, my mind did entertain.

And I knew it was true

Catching sound of Nightingale's refrain

Oh, how I love this liberation . . .

Knowing that I too, must return to civilization.

CLOUD MOODS
(Dark Brooding Day)

Black threatening mass of turbulent strength . . .

Throw tumultuous crackle across the dark hell-heaven sky.

And shoot your fire daggers down—mercilessly to the ground.

Burn the Motherload with Father-Almighty fist.

Spew your sheets of sleet and rocks of ice.

Wreak havoc of flood and mud.

Traverse your tantrum-driven path,

Certain that nothing and no one escapes

Your pent-up capricious wrath.

CLOUD MOODS
(Clear Happy Day)

White puff of fluff-cumulus . . .

Float and fly, light and high

In your bright dominion of sky.

Rock me gently on your heavenly-soft bed.

Embellish the blue with your wispy, nebulous

Patchwork of feather-white hue.

Travel to where you go—and know

You are earth's irrigation,

Sunset enhancement,

And day-dream romancer.

DAWN OF THE SURREAL

The stars gave way

    to a

Sentinel of silhouetted palm trees . . .

A transcendent escort,

Leading to a grand meadow

In a mixed pastel sherbet sky . . .

    of

Soft tangerine, creme, canary,

And wisp of blue-nebulous hue;

Embellished with crested cameo Moon.

    All . . .

Slipping silently behind a translucent curtain

To another dominion.

POINT OF DISCOVERY

I'm full-up with half emptiness.

Tired of the uninspired—

Livid with rampant mediocrity.

Urgency presses me to feed to a glut—

Suck Mother Life's milk . . .

Raw and unpasteurized,

Rife with ravage of hideous infection.

The blister-blemished consequence, of venture . . .

A pock-marked legacy, for having lived.

Wrung experienced guts,

Surface in the pores of our make-up.

A face more attractive . . .

Than is that of the oblivious.

DUAL B'S

A bitch and a bastard spout accusations in provocation dastard.

The exchange bent on hurt and debase . . .

A maleficence of disgrace.

Vicious ripping and tearing—

Tooth and nail have they entered their hell.

No semblance of dignity, this odious display . . . ignorantly.

One, no more valid than the other.

One, no more amiable than the other.

For they are Bitch and Bastard.

On this level, they shall shout their story . . .

Both cursed cursing couples condemned to the confines

   OF PURGATORY

MASK

A seductress peeled away makeup

Layer by layer;

To reveal the mask

Of her foundation.

THE AMERICAN DREAM

The American dream?

Oh, it's found in a land deed . . .

But, the variable-rate mortgages gouges until I bleed.

The American dream?

Oh, it's equal education opportunity . . .

But, look at the substandard schools in the community.

The American dream? Oh, it's Social Security . . .

But, entitlement funds are a scarcity.

The American dream? Oh, close your eyes and fantasize.

DREAM PURSUIT

Sprint your endomorph
Soaked dream course.

Blood vessels convulse,
Hyper-excite to
Accelerated pulse.

Expectant elongated limbs-longing
Stretched to break. Nerve fatigue . . . never ending.

Gap closing there . . .
Gasp of rarified air,
Oxygenated dream affair,
Grope-grasp for the elusive Golden Ring . . .
A coat tail offering . . . fleeting.

Lunge for the thing—
Coat tail crumble and disintegrate.
The object of venerate . . .
The source of frustrate.
Flapping shreds of threads,
Wind-blown mocking muse—
The escape art of vanished abuse.

Club of guarded admissions—
Into the inner sanctum pressed this run.
Next time . . .

There will be fruition.

THE NARCISSIST

Odious faceless creatures
Taken with themselves,
Are found everywhere
Masturbating in immodest streets.

The naked narcissists sport smug smirks
Of the self-indulgent.
Astride their buff behinds,
A belligerent monkey clings—mockingly.

The unclad, uncouth . . . on oblivious verge
Of secretion inundation—
Swept away by their own sticky-slick bio river flow.

Torsos and egos traverse and converge,
Down a slime slippery street,
To where the gutters meet.
All, seeking sublimation,
Each preoccupied with self gratification.

SPHERE OF INFLUENCE

Oh, how I'd love to play with that

Voluminous ass.

To race and chase

Her buoyant-elusive fully inflated

Beach ball . . .

Firm, and luscious and round.

To tackle it and roll around the ground;

Its smooth, semi-seemless surface

Sizzling to the touch . . .

Flaunting a pink crevice.

To press her sphere

Against my happy cheek,

Warm and pliant;

Then, lay deliriously spent.

ORIFICE

A wet fold of flesh

Has the brain enmeshed.

Pink jaws clasp, clamp, and squeeze.

Extracting.

Drop . . . drop . . . drained.

ODE TO EXPLORATION

There are places he wished he'd been . . .

Locations in exotic environs.

Eluded—gone unexplored,

Those special spots,

Where the sun shines not.

Oh, to probe the narrow gorge—

The crevice folds,

The sloping curves of the grassy mound,

The perfect hideaway might he have found . . .

Her long lean loins wrapped around.

THE OLE IN AND OUT . . .

The ole in and out . . .

Most sublime pleasure beyond doubt.

Male and female,

Yin enjoying yang.

Wet membrane a-thrill with the exchange.

Instinct primordial-base delight . . .

Soft muscle

In concert with

Hard and upright.

"Can't live with . . . Can't live without."

Surreptitious reference to . . .

The ole in and out.

AROUSAL

Oh how they thrive on turbulence . . .

Excited, frenzied disturbance.

A sneer is challenge to torn veneer . . .

Laid open raw flesh, wet-wounded sweet smell

Of freshly drawn blood, oozing sick delight.

Roll and revel in passion aroused fight.

Then unite in the night's dark finale . . .

Genitals meshed and caressed in hot crescendo

To make sane, the chilling inane soiree.

FIRE PASSION

Eroticism of the hearth . . .
Flames flicking, licking, elongating up;
Deep into the heart of an imaginative libido.

Love solo, or music a la mode . . .
Golden, inviting, repelling—ever changing fickle splendor—
Penchant to turn and burn the over-enamored fondle.

Capricious comforter—warmth provider, tantrum throw . . .
Burn to a seductive-mystical fantasia glow,
Your amber allure of incandescent love, spent inanimate.

Desirous of your fervent love frolic within your torrid
environ . . .
But, your response I can well imagine . . .
Never granted.

Your unrequited amour
Unattainable, now and ever more . . .
Ardor unexplored.

RELAXED PRESENTMENT

Had myself a miraculous, scintillating experience—
Bordering on the lascivious.

On holiday in a most alluring place—
Arid, on the cusp of fertile mountain scape . . .
Relaxed, my mind traveled to come upon
A myriad of delicious presentments;
Virtual candy box assortment of erotic succulents,
Of human genitalia resemblance.

Utterly sensual—
The Prickly Pear,
The Yucca,
The Peyote,
Cactus formed to phallus.

Self questioned:
Was I "tuned in."
        Or
Gone over the "deep end."

I shook my head vigorously—
To rid myself of the unseemly.

But again, mind registration of nudity—
Nature in the raw . . . in the fullest figurative sense;
A special environ *endowment.*

Mountainous prostrations as far as the eye could see—
A stretch of credulity!

Row after row . . .
Fold after fold . . .
Crevice after crevice . . .

Sprinkled with grass—evocative of pubis.
Sun played upon, cast deep shadow throws
Between the lean loins of this harem;
An assemblage to rival that of the world's most wealthy suntans.

This, the run of an over active imagination?
The hallucinations of a sick mind?

Perhaps, this fault you may in this account find.
To my mind, I'd rather prefer this to be
Sensory heightened reality—
Lovely in presentment and purity.

NUPTIALS

Wed if you choose,
But spare those cursed vows . . .
Slaughter that sacred cow.

Cut off its bloody head at the neck.
Better this sacrifice,
Than shame of having showered in rice.

The times, find these platitudes archaic,
Personal constitution is concern of greater stake.

Self fulfillment within the combine . . .
A relevant release—
When free to be . . . Forefront of mind.

TRIVIAL PLAY

Come, let play with imps.
Long and hard your acrobatics—
A carnal obsession with tricks.

Time shall query your sanity mad hatter
But now, your prowess need flatter,
And the moment is of paramount matter.

And time will surely inquire again . . .
Somewhere near the end.
But now, no need for reply with haste.
The substance of your story
Is etched upon your
Crazed-characterless face.

SMALL WONDER

Top of the mourn . . . a face admonishes "do not disturb,"

A pair of eyes avert to avoid intrusion,

And a head sports electronic ear plugs—

To the ultimate exclusion.

In search of sanity, I run toward the sea shore.

People sit isolated in vehicles and nearly make of me a gore.

Despondency propels me ever faster towards the sanctity of the sea.

A wave crashes the sand and a faceless woman emerges from its spray.

Across the dual protrusion of her sweat shirt . . .

Bold embossed letters loudly proclaimed and shouted:

"TIGHT"

And I wondered if she was . . .

Or if someone cared . . .

And had anyone been there.

DIFFERENCE AND INDIFFERENCE

An uncomely girl sat across from me in the airport lobby.

Her behavior interesting, if not appalling.

In truth, I found it most enthralling.

She opened and closed her thighs rapidly . . .

Stretching taught her mini-skirt,

Then, snapping it back . . .

Like a rubberband.

This, while men rushed by with suitcase in hand.

Several minutes elapsed

And more men passed by,

But her conduct failed to attract another curious eye.

Now, I was intrigued by the exhibition.

Was it sexual invitation or a nervous condition?

A pretty flight attendant's smile snatched my attention.

I boarded the plane reflecting upon the difference . . .

And the indifference.

PIECE ANATOMY

Silly-scary,
When a man falls in love with
Parts of a woman's anatomy.

The lewd languish over legs . . .
The vile venerate of vagina . . .
The obscene ogle of breasts . . .
The asinine fuss over ass . . .
The hideous hype of hair . . .
The salivate over plump lips . . .

The need to come to grips
With what men can be,
And what a woman should be.

If she's not loved in her entirety,
She ain't loved completely.

CRITICAL REVIEW

Sit down to a table set with plate of meat.

A dead carcass you venture to eat;

Flesh traumatized, tortured and beat.

Envision the plight of your unwholesome treat:

Caged chicken arthritis stricken . . .

Beef grown of ingested hormones,

And trichinosis pork enticing your fork.

Poor Souse!

The blood of innocent lambs stain your mouth.

FREEWAY

A broken line deliniates the zone of your continuance.

While mega-ton machines barrel about—

Some with brakes and shoes . . . some without.

It's tough getting from here to there . . .

Especially now that no one has time to spare.

Peddle to the floor—you otherwise non-aggressor.

This is your great battle . . . your commuter war.

Take heed! the counter forces close rank and surround.

Straight ahead, a fire of tail lights threaten.

The warrior on your right is an open-wounded divorcee.

The combatant on the left, a shell-shocked job terminated.

 Damnation—your rear is assaulted!

AUTO

A hard metal box

Sits, suffering the sweltering heat;

Belly bursting liquid viscose . . .

Veins pumping juices vaporous . . .

Legs elasticized in mushy mounds . . .

    Poor powerpack

Slave clump of steel,

Readying itself for the most severe reduction . . .

The hellish experience of

Internal combustion.

DRUNKARDS

Curious, is the way crazed-wounded
Parts of cars seem to be in search
Of another hapless encounter;

Longing to rub-up against
Another naive, unsuspecting
Petrol drinking maniacal vehicle.

ODE TO L.A.

Los Angeles—Look east of Western . . . you'll find Olympic is
Korea, and Pico is Mexico . . .
Curious barios neighborhooded—I once knew, but can scarcely
say I know.

O. and P.—Parallel boulevards in opposition.
Culturally divergent and never convergent,
They are separated ethnos . . . a nation's micro-pathos;
Sovereigns on separate streets
That do not and will not ever meet.

Assimilation is violation, and violence is assumed
In shanty towns that boast store front signs
Intelligible only to the new-American.

Immigration yes! orientation no.
Is that how it goes? Or perhaps worse, is it the reverse?

Korea-Olympic, Mexico-Pico—Let your roads run intersecting
Aspirations.
The present direction leads to a dead end destination . . .

A DECEASED NATION.

CITY WALK

Strolled into the belly of the inner city,
To woefully witness everywhere . . .
Drunk-tilted structures reeling
From the hangover of neglect—
Strained to stand erect.

Windows askew—recessed in dark sunken sockets—
Image flash of face fleeting—
Not wanting to be seen . . .
Momentarily frozen in shocking resemblance—
Windowpane/face-frame semblance.

Nowhere was this cesspool non-reflective—
Ripple effected excremental droppings,
Decomposing a ghetto.

Row after row of decay and stench
Of gut wrench squalor.

Sidewalks violent volcanic erupted
To a hazardous negotiate of convex concrete roller coaster scape.
Streets pot-holed and rain saturated,
Sport a myriad of minor lakes and streams—
Deep trenched, traversed to their shores . . .
Scars born of isolation, exclusion, and indifference.

Remnants of an ongoing silent conflagration—
In competition with recurrent echo
Of the gang-related audible one.

Come nightfall,
All sorts of vermin sliver through the cracks;
To exact their measure of pleasure . . .
The rats, roaches, dope pushers, and high-heeled hookers.

Therein lies the despair
Found in the bloated, malnourished belly of the inner city.

An insignificant bludgeoned bleeding body . . .
Face down and out—
Defeated of multiple open scab-encrusted eye sores.

Examined in its entire enormity . . .
A Goliath sector of neglect.
Left abandoned—
In red colored reckless hemorrhagic torrents of blood,
Running swiftly . . . unabatedly,
Into the center of your *uncolored neighborhoods*.

FROM BABY TO BUM

He stepped up to me
Feeble and frail.

His body reeked of a decomposed carcass.
His breath smelled of stagnant sewers.

The innocence of a child
Shone in his baby-blue eyes.

I ventured to hug him—
Stopped short . . .
And cried.

HOMELESSNESS

What is to be made of this sad affair?
People homeless, left babbling in our streets everywhere.
Come, this cannot be fair—
The multitude in wretched despair.

Eyes avert to stem hurt,
With self-deception of mirth;
While the caring ponder its commentary on society's worth.

What does this condition grievous say about us?
If a body is only as healthy as its ailing organ,
Then thinking folk must move to stop this chagrin.

Decency and conscience is what's needed
In regard to our "base element."
To ignore the relevance is morally abhorrent and a slimy
wallow in decadence.

REFLECTION

What is this reflected image I see . . .

A distorted collage of parity,

Or, simply reality?

Guess one never knows,

Unable to directly peer

Into one's pose.

DOMINATOR

CONTROLLING, DOMINATING TWIT! . . .

TAKE ME FOR A NITWIT?

Drive home your point . . . but, better not miss.

Your dagger may find its target in ironic twist;

A self-inflicted wound fatal to the hilt.

The red-run of your persuasion split.

A relationship-terminal, severed beyond tact.

This blade you cannot extract,

Those words, beyond your retract.

INANE EXCHANGE

"You're not handicapped"
The suspicious yuppies verbally
Shot at the human, driven to a blue parking spot.

"Some people drive up and take advantage."
Continued the onslaught.

As the handicapped man exited his car—
With aid of his cane,
This apt retort:

"Some people *sit*, and take advantage."

To this, there was no refute.
The yuppie-hushed mouths were handily capped—mute.

PASSING THROUGH

Property we claim to own is neither yours nor mine.

Better to know that we are merely borrowers

Of Earth and time.

Instinctively, we are driven to possess,

Fear and greed supplant the best.

Build your fortress to protect life's accumulations,

But will it be strong enough to hold back

The would-be tide of violation?

Paranoia robs your peace—

Think of life as a temporary lease.

ENCOUNTER

I heard the creaking open of his door

As I simultaneously did the same.

I did not want to bother him,

But he was equally curiosity driven.

We stood silently in the respective doorways of our apartments,

Each awaiting the other's exit.

Urgency and impatience got the better of us.

In unison, we peered around our portals . . .

Eyes trapped in absurdity.

THE IMBALANCE

Golden Boy's
Voracious feed on steroids
To flaunt an enormous muscle pump,
Is beset with mental muscle shriveled and shrunk—

Starvation/neglect . . . a midget intellect.

Gilded luster tarnished . . .
To an impoverished swagger,
Teetering from the weight of his body's

Imbalance.

POWER PEOPLE

Power people . . . Assets and position hoarded.

Hold on with fearful grip,

Paranoid of potential slip.

Big unto themselves, but pathetically thin

Within the grand arena of compassionate life.

Shared pieces of self conjures despair and strife.

A perception exists, that with generosity comes
disappearance—

So fragile is the foundation of their existence.

Little guy, be mindful of others and create your own.

Yours, surely will be the more lavish throne.

CINEMA PSYCHOSIS

Preen ye Kings and Queens

Of the big screen;

No matter that fame is fleeting—

Your eminence largely

Of minimal meaning.

But alas,

Public adoration is Camelot—

Without which,

Regal egos rot.

EGO LINE

No wonder

Entertainers place themselves

Ego-forefront . . . sublime.

They have but to look at the poor doting fool

Who stands anticipant, at the far rear

Of their show's performance line.

PRIVILEGED CLASS

A silver-coated ball of pampered Persian
Cat-fluff, rhinestone collar-cuffed,
Sat contentedly plump, in a purple
Storefront, with yellow window trim.

Licking and preening . . .
He or she blissfully entrenched in aristocracy—
Impervious to the hardships of the majority.

DICHOTOMY

Social Puritans we are . . .

Sex-sick indulgents

Nauseous from a glut of nudity

And offended by the human form.

Lamentable is this sorrowful assemblage

Of influence driven chattel of hypocrisy—

Slaves to mass conformity.

Entranced by images in celluloid or TV.

Zombies speaking and walking upright . . .

The babbling vanquished

And buried conquests of civility—

Severed from reality

Vis-a-vis vicarious cinematic fantasy.

SOCIAL BUTTERFLY

Goodbye, my petite social butterfly.

Flit and flirt . . .

From bud to stem to dirt . . .

Alight upon other's mate

In a frenzy to copulate.

Go about tempting fate . . .

As you cross-pollinate.

Dance light and airy . . .

Substance made a mockery.

Dawn will cast a deep shadow

On your foreshortened sensitivity . . .

Highlight to a life of meaningless brevity.

TRIGONOMETRY

Three is the worst number there can be . . .

An unholy trinity.

She, she and he . . .

A triangle of perversity.

Inevitably, one will see, and leave the two to be.

In all probability,

The insipid affair leaving one in desperate need of repair,

And a wretched pair left in calamitous air.

PENSIVE

A choice was made today . . .

To set right the disarray.

Two women profess their love for me . . .

But, with only one can there a union be.

Sympathy for the rejected . . .

Her deep feelings most certainly respected.

Alas . . . a decision is sound if serenity be found,

An explanation sought, need not be given . . .

For self endearment have I striven.

No finger pointing ravished . . .

For we all do our best with burdensome baggage.

MYSTIQUE

Woman . . .

What's behind those eyes
Set in perplexed guise,
Sunk amid cranial frame . . .
Semblance of same humanness—
The antithesis of man . . .
Channel to attract with positive polarity—
Alternate current flow,
To repel through negative eccentricity.

Drive your emotional coupe of bemuse . . .
The two seated vehicle
You've fitted with neurotic abuse.
Metamorphose from human to insect insidious.
Mix your fermented sweet and sour elixir.

Venerable venomous Black Widow,
Press naive prey beneath blood-scented red hour glass.
Seize his ass!
Anesthetize with smell of your sex.
Take your pleasure . . .
Man is not your measure.

Male . . . mundane, inane, emotionally restrained . . .
Desirous of being left alone
But, his libido you own.

Never to be understood by man,
You are the irresistible force
Within the Grand Plan,
The progenitor of procreation,
And agitation that begs
Insatiable manipulation.

Possessor of power elite,
You are quandary of mystique . . .
Conspirator of secrets,
The content of which
Only the Gods are privileged to speak.

BEACON WOMAN

Woman . . . house of light, beacon in the night,

And haven for beleaguered vessels—

Cast your hypnotic beam.

Draw hither the loosely tethered, hopeless adrift,

And the seemingly free.

Pull them into the lap of your lascivious port.

Powdered and scented, manicured nails,

And styled coif of tiles . . .

All primed and painted—

Facade of features accentuated.

Provocative is your sweet guile.

Smile your bright-blinding luminance,

Only a few souls have the experience to know . . .

You and your allure are largely

OPTICAL DELUSIONAL.

BRIGITTE

Who is la femme there . . . moves with sophisticated aire?

Passionate—Obstinate . . . Slender she is to Sleek—

Tanned like teak.

Ah, but to hear her speak . . .

Franco Melodic

Sounds of sonnet sweet, her lips mine yearn to meet.

And this, a mere morsel of the exotic whole:

Italian ire stoked by passion-fire—

Born of soul-heat Afrique.

La femme there? Elle est tres chick . . . L'exquisite—

Ma Brigitte.

PRINCESS

Content to stay at home . . .
Pretty kept thing.

Pray to *YOUR GOD*,
That you are never found wanting.

FIRE

Flicker and flirt

A *pas de deux* . . .

Ballerina of the hearth.

Warm, tease and excite . . .

Diminish to a relaxed incandescent glow.

Irresistible is your inviting, enticing encore . . .

Elicits craving for more.

But, you are not to be possessed . . .

Forbidden to caress.

The seduced-stubborn . . .

Get burned.

LOVE EMBRACE

Embrace the love that is there . . .
Savor your fortune . . .
Not found everywhere.

Rare, is a compatible blend
Of man and woman;

Soul-mated friends
Come together through
Cosmic energy extend.

Life-long companions
In this one life certain,
Navigating environs uncertain.

Constantly evolving . . .
Problem solving . . .
Not a harnessed team,
Rather,
The free gleam,
In pairs of eyes
Love recognized.

SLIP DRIFT

"Hey buddy, here's the drift . . .

Once into her you slip—

There is ownership."

WALKURIAN NIGHTMARE

Other worldly,
Is this tantalizing She-Beast . . .

Feasts on man—
Chews him up . . . to upchuck . . .
Chunks of undigested remains,
Turns, to seek more of the same.

Insatiable, this glut for more and more
Putrid male fetish feast,

For she is She-Beast,
Voracious hell-sent Aphrodite of vicious-sick appetite.

Try to fight . . .
The struggle is of no use—
You're in a Vaginal noose.

His constricted libido is hers—your demise,
To nosh between merciless bloody molars and aching thighs.

Jazz

Brain impulse overload—to explode,
Igniting blood, body, and bones
In searing syncopation,
Amid an incandescent improvisation;

A scintillating ride.
Seat-buckled astride agile instruments—
Carrying me giddy, to somewhere uncertain . . .
Unknown . . . unrecognized—delightfully surprised.

Senses found crashed down—looped around . . .
Thrill maneuvered,
Exhilarant . . . spent, transcendent—
Emotionally gamut wrung.

Straight line conduit to the human spirit—
Avant-garde elevated to the echelon.
Glowing red-hot in this galaxy . . . and beyond.

THE TUNNEL

Scarcely recognized the outside.
Attribute to my doctor's behest
Of two weeks bed rest.

Upon arising from this much needed repose,
The door to a heretofore unseen world flew open,
Beckoning me to come have a *look-see.*

With fixed gaze, I surveyed a poverty of mass malaise.
Like a creeping haze, slowly suffocating . . . debilitating—
Everything.

In stunned, shocked quandary
I sought to determine how and why
Was I suddenly able to perceive this malady;
To "see the light"—
Possible benefit of prescribed bed rest of a fortnight?

Set out on foot to further explore—
Found to my horror, a pervasive stagnation;
Creativity and innovation ebbed to desolation.

Cracked, barren land—and man in the very same condition.
Alarming was the apparent lack of will to identify
And fight this seamy scourge.

Indeed, some seemed resigned,
While others seemed to revel in the mire—
Perversely invigorated with the distortion of man;

Salivating with prospect of exploit and profit taking—
The proceeds of slick-trick manipulation . . .
Finds the programmed masses, parading in a
One million abreast robotic march,
Into the black tunnel of mediocrity—
All, functioning in fear of fellow robot peer pressure.

Nowhere, was this festering infection more evident,
Than among the decimated youth;

Children seemed to have an innate sense of the uncouth;
With powerless recognition comes a slow death—
Wilted before maturity.

The pseudo-stimulation of pyrotechnics and cybernetics,
Has them lost—adrift in a vast void, languid—without purpose,
Tethered to the nebulous . . . removed from terra firma.

This was revealed to me . . .
I'm awake—not dreaming;
A nightmare there—for all human beings.
A rainbow of hope . . .
Lies with the deviates not yet robot wired,
Those who will not acquiesce to the substandard
Of the hell-lost insensitive, and mired uninspired.

PERSONAL MERIT

Tiresome is talk of acceptance of groups ethnic

Or otherwise.

Triumphant are those individuals connected

By a mutual recognition of fine human traits—

The source where endearment ought be derived.

Singular acknowledgment . . . one on one—

Not the remedy of a jaundiced hypocrisy

Administered to bandage those societies

Poisoned and ill-run.

A MOTHER

A mother is everything we want her to be.

And, one day we see what she is in reality:

Loving, nurturing, supportive, and—

Human.

She never claimed to be a saint.

This distorted picture we chose to paint.

Above all, mother provided a womb.

Deep down, it's where our souls lie—

Could they be exhumed.

FAMILY

Blood heritage is often the source of great disparage;

Anticipation of conduct expected,

With culture acquiescence affected.

Step away from behavior acceptable . . .

You are deemed objectionable.

Long-toothed, loose-tongued conformists

Bite your back.

Courageously, you deflect the attack.

Bravo Maverick!

Victimized and ostracized, you escape emotional tatter,

And sport a personal strength character

That is of greater matter.

CURTAINS

Appealing was she . . .
Standing . . . waiting to be received;

While masculine eyes thrived upon her person.

A surprise to their aroused male pride!
Presently, the lovely was presented with a bouquet . . .
Suitor enter, of the same gender.

Darkness!
Curtain fell on this vignette . . .

Masculine splendor fantasy . . .
Segued to . . .
"Forget it."

D e s e r t

Listen to the voice of the desert . . .

Its parched throat, cracked

Crying and pleading for moisture.

A hot-tempered wind,

chasing the hyperactive tumbleweed

Across searing silica sand;

Sadistically humored by replies flashing

Between crevices of rock.

A buzzard circles above.

A desperate mind

Finds false relief

In a fabricated

Cool-water oasis;

As heat waves

Rise and crash

On its shore.

THE CAMEL

Funny, uncomely creature
Of one or two humps . . .
You've taken your lumps.

Misunderstood, maligned, and criticized—
No wonder disdain often fills
Your suffering eyes.

Never quite tame,
The kick and bite and spit
Of animal inane.

Unwilling beast of burden . . .
Used by Bedouin—
Devoid of affection for man;

Fill-up your digest-diverse, thirst suppressed stomach;
You cantankerous desert belly-rust!
Lope and plod along
Under long desert-hot sun.

And know that for five thousand years
You've survived without peers.
Unique . . .
Absent your stamina, resolve, and courage—
No quit, no tire,
Nomads would have perished
Under the onslaught of desert fire.

Although lacking the horse's grace,
No man can look you in the face,
And fail to admire the hardships
Brethren endured,
In mutual quest of life sustenance assured.

THE ARABIAN

If ever an equine deserved to be deemed of royalty . . .

It would be thee;

For no other is so richly worthy.

The Bedouin owner of horse of your blood line,

Esteemed you divine—a grand compliment,

And set up shelter with you in his tent

Your value beyond estimate . . .

Warrior with stamina unspent,

High-spirited legs afire,

you are last of breeds to tire.

Throughout Arabia and the entire Middle East,

There is no other mount can so favorably compete.

To sit astride your finely configured Arabian frame,

Slice through the wind . . . sword drawn for attack,

There is no more exhilarating ride upon a prouder back.

ROYAL BIRDS

Winged majestic creature of heaven almight,

Splendidly light is your marvel aflight.

Feathered plume attuned with the wind—

Up-drafted to soar round again.

Motionless . . . master of the sky,

Surveyor of all earth-bound species below.

No hollow beyond find—

Your vision so highly refined.

Folding feathers for fearless fall of accuracy uncanny . . .

Targeted prey at mercy.

Of royal blood are these birds upon higher echelon . . .

THE EAGLE, THE HAWK, and THE FALCON

THE LOCQUACIOUS

A band of juvenile chimpanzees
Chose to Chit and chat and chuckle,
At the expense of a wise ole monkey;
Who appeared to be bored and fatigued.

Presently,

A beautiful bunch of bananas
Came cascading down a tree,
Plopped in the midst of the chimps and lone monkey;
Triggering savage salivating scamper for the fare.

Naturally, the young chimps were first to get there;
Beating the ole monkey to the feast.
But, their talk-tired jaws
Would not allow them to eat.

The wise ole primate
Strolled up . . . cool and mellow,
Grabbed the creamy yellow,
And laughed at the gibber-prone fellows.

Try as hard as they could to protest . . .
It was useless—
Jaws locked from lack of rest.

The intelligent monkey turned and departed
With a singular jeer:

"Invariably you lose my muse,
When incessant chatter you choose."

ELEPHANT

Rough-dried cracked hide burly beast,
Sport your magnificent ivory tusks—
Stave off poachers wealth . . .
Trumpet your health . . .

For you are Goliath of nature's creatures;
Curiously agile and sure-footed
For animal your size.

Your list of enemies, only man comprised.
Survived . . .
Despite the maniacs' sick aphrodisiac thirst-thrive.

So, swing and sway—
Be on your hungered way
To your quarter ton nutrients per day.

But, bear in mind . . .
Your memory so fine—

The earth's inhabitants are multiplying
With prolific food insistence—
Do your best,
Not to eat yourselves out of existence.

NIGHT PREDATOR

Night falls

With wild predatorial call
   Of
Animals foraging with torch-lit focus.

To ravage traversed rich, and barren land.

Slither and slide . . .

Element of stealth and surprise,

To pounce upon the unsuspecting—before sunrise.

A shrill death-scream rips the ears

Of prey that got away.

A KILL! . . .

Another completion of a morbid mission . . .
   Via
The merciless, calculating devil incarnate . . .

The upright, two-legged human primate.

HUMMINGBIRD

Adorably cute mystery . . . half bird, part bee.

Silent are thee . . .

Never obtrusive—always elusive.

Sit still for just one moment of continual hover . . .

For I am enamored lover . . .

Enthralled by the delicacy of your exquisite beauty.

Feathered plume I see . . .

Exceeds everything earthly . . .

Disposed to heavenly.

A variation of color that surpasses the peacock.

But vain . . .

You are not.

Flash the spectrum of the rainbow . . .

Then off you go . . .

To only heaven knows.

Saber-like beak . . .

Nature's gift for sweet nectar you extract . . .

Never for bitter attack.

Little Hummingbird,

Dart from rose to hibiscus . . .

And know that you are loved for your . . .

Deus existence.

THE STRANGER

Finally . . . forced to look upon yourself;

To peer into the stranger

Unfamiliar to you—

Introspection long overdue.

The revelation tugs at your guts.

Scrutiny begun,

Your impulse is to turn and run.

From what?
From whom?

The truth comes . . .

That, that someone,

Is alien to the other one.

CHAIN LINKED

A heavy chain burdens my shoulders and neck,
Pressing deep into my flesh.
Thick oppressive alloy links . . .
Comprised of Time and Money.

Time and Money . . .
Imbalanced compositions—
Cumbersome, continuous, interconnected
Dark circles—etched depression,
Pain and anxiety . . .
A suffocating strangle-hold of currency
Around finite longevity.
Agony.

Shed the shackles—
Chuck it all, and be done!
Lay down . . . cry, and say goodbye.

Then, possessed by whim . . .
Haunted by the proverbial dream,
And dogged by
Constant comparison of irrelevant riches.
Prostitute and bitches . . .
Forever chain linked to Time and Money

COIN SEGMENT

CLINK . . . a coin is collected.

CLINK . . . a coin is respected.

CLINK . . . a coin is protected.

CLICK . . . a second has passed.

CLICK . . . an hour has elapsed.

CLICK . . . a life has expired.

TRANSITION

Stayed . . . Motionless . . . catatonic—

   Depressed

The sky . . . mood supportive

   Dark-motionless

Pervasive gloom—forbode of doom
Bolt of thunder jolts the room.
A tandem of misery . . .
Accompanied pathos apropos:
Heaven anguished, and Hell ravished—
Both on brink of burst
Into a billion precipitant particles.
Pent-up anger . . . deluge begun—
Pounding . . . pulverizing . . . agonizing
Break-down run—
Stretch of electrod sanity . . .
Spent elasticity—
Faltering grop for reality . . .
Plead for smattering of normalcy.

   Pity . . .

Unable to be undone.
No one can alleviate—
Eradicate this personification
Of *GONE*.
Patience outside and beyond.

A patient commended to Almighty hands
And the peace that accompanies God's Environ.

ELECTION DAY

Consider the significance to posterity
When a candidate claims victory.
With final tally . . .
Comes triumph and tragedy.
Elation and exultation of dual degree . . .
The elected and the electorate
Basking in a slightly-sick . . . sadistic glory.
The defeated . . . humiliated publicly,
Is given to banishment psyche.

Rally enthusiasm after the fray,
Posturing and swaggering . . .
In despicable display.
Little thought accorded the overpowered
On this triumphant day.

The defeated, dejected and in devastated dismay.
Go ahead and play!
Forget about the guy who died today.

With rout, hopefully comes recovery.
But, why the concern for the trounced,
Who's savvy ought to be based in practical reality?
With a loser looms a probably despondency.
Politician Be forgot . . .
A human in debased condition
Is deserving of some extent of compassion.
In the interim,
There is a correlation to posterity
As relates to . . .
The victor and the vanquished
And the health of . . .
A Nation's psyche at test.

TAX MAN

Once again . . .
The Revenue Man
Extends his leech-encrusted
Beggars hand.

Wish he'd leave me a little of mine.
Perhaps he ought seek out others of his kind—
Find a bread line.

Join his fellow hapless, down and out—
Therein lies camaraderie . . . a fraternity
And his Social Security.

WALL STREET

Wall Street has me beat . . .
My soul replete
With the bleeding wounds of defeat.

The ticker tape mockingly proclaims my fate—
I must capitulate.

Ego feed, or was it greed?

Wait!

News of an employee purge . . . a company merge—
Possible point surge!

Fortune *must* emerge.

CREDIT CRUNCH

Lenders and Borrowers
Are the financial interactive
    Reduced.

The former,
The abusive obscene;

The latter,
The duped demeaned.

A gouge, glut-feast
Plate dripping fat-filled Interest Rate.

Bank employed, masked robber barons,
Armed with a bastardization of the American Dream
To own everything—instantly;
And a surreptitious fine printed promissory note . . .
An oppressive loan float.

Groveling, sniveling snakes!
Bask in the shaded glory of your ill-gotten gains.
Pray to God,
There be absolution for your odious remains.

As for you,
The perennial cheated fools . . .
Yours, is a sorrowful woe.

Toe to toe with prosperity,
Carrot-bated quest for the golden ring . . .
A deluded standard of living—
Debt ridden with *things* . . .
Collections material—
Further removed from the ethereal.

CRYSTALLINE

Love those days that appear in rare beauty . . .

With crystalline clarity.

Everything juxtaposed into the surreal . . .

In contrast with the pollutant distorted real.

Allow me to step into this fair world every day . . .

For this, Any fare, I'd eagerly pay.

MESSAGE FOR THE MILLENNIUM

They're out there . . .
Watching, reveling, awaiting crisis critical;
Signal for decent.
Extraterrestrials humored by human maleficence and discontent.
Witness to violence and senseless conflict.

A smile . . . no, . . . a smirk;
Rudiment reaction to Earth gone berserk.
We lowly developed inhabitants—
Light-years away from enlightenment . . .
Third planet from the Sun,
Another dark solar system
Ripe sphere for seizure and colonialism.
Entities locked in derision and dissension,
Accelerating the universal forces of exploitation.

Survival is contingent upon
Conciliation, co-habitation, and the understanding
Of the fundamental essential that there be unification.
Failing this . . .
We are Earthlings extinct—
Doomed to alien invasion
And universal conflagration.

WAKE UP CALL
  (a message)

Today . . .
A dragonfly buzzed and clipped my ear,
A bird's wing taunted and slapped my face,
And a bumble bee was possessed to sting.

Made me stop to question
If there was to all this . . .
Some meaning.

Could it be that finally
They all have had enough—
Not willing to take anymore of
Man's stuff?
A silly thought . . .
Ought to be dismissed.

Until just now . . . this!

A flock of gulls commensed
A bomb-dive from the sky.
Surrounded was I.
These foul creatures,
Bent on deforming my facial features.

Screaming and flailing . . .
Mad out of my mind,
A stick I did fortunately find.
Swinging at the crazed devils with all my might,
They seemed to know no fright.
Blood fell from the air
And splattered everywhere.

The sky appeared to open . . .
They departed.
I looked at my bloodied hand . . .

A red trail led to the sand.

To my edification and horror . . .
A blood-red message stated:

Wake up mankind—
Earth is to be shared with all living creatures.
If this, you do not soon learn,
We shall be your teachers.

IT'S COMING!

Something is about to happen . . .

Something is brewing . . .

And it's gonna be powerful!

Hurricane—torrential rain—earth tremble . . .

A rising crescendo of calamity . . .

Amassing . . . amassing.

I know it, I feel it, see it in Fido's eyes,

I can do nothing to prevent it . . .

Impotent . . .

Curled-up fetal—

Protecting my Balls.

SHAKEN

"It happened today,
The big one arrived—
And I survived!

There was no warning,
Just a faint tinkling sound—
Like ice cubes vigorously shaken in a glass.

I'd prefer it had been a break-in intruder,
Fix'n himself a drink—

What the hell, may as well climb over the rubble
And mix a martini.

To my horror,
A stranger lay by the refrigerator—
Skull crushed, clutching a glass of vodka and vermouth.

Shaken . . . not stirred."

FALLING LEAVES

Streams of light beamed
Between the unoccupied limbs
Of an Autumn Maple Tree.

Unexpectedly,
An avalanche of leaves
Commenced to snow upon me.
Petals floating gently . . .
Ticking my face—
Landing purposefully at my feet.

Rid yourself of this inundation
My mind did entreat;
Buried up to the neck in a leafy sleet.

Perceiving a sordid fate,
A frantic struggle to extricate . . .
I did initiate.

The leafage tightened and entwined the mind;
Constricted—straight jacketed
      With
Suffocating, breath shortening apprehension.

Overwhelmed, the horrors of death did confront me.
Frantically thrashing to a fatigue,
My body acquiesced . . .
Relaxed and fell asleep
In a bed of Autumn's heaven.

SPRING

Spring has sprung . . .
The groundhog flashed his elusive head . . .
Appalled to see a shadow solo—
Unembellished by a mate,
Ran, in pursuit of an altered fate.

And,

A fellow primate, fell victim to some kind of restless fever . . .
An unexplainable fervor to let loose and explore,
Leapt to scratch an itch . . .
To tap into the new, and experience more.

Love Doves,
Driven in cooperative search for twigs
To construct a sanctum—
Sensuous, lazy lay-around
Until a full nest they've found.

Butterflies,
Flitter, saddled astride . . .
Dance in and out of
Sun drenched flower beds,
Dazzled with the pleasure
That travels through their heads.

Spring has sprung . . .

Everyone hooked up in interlock
Of seasonal sublime state . . .
Insects, birds, and primates
Enjoying nature's tantalizing plate:

An appetizer to salivate and hormone race,
An entree to self proliferate,

A dessert . . . the warmth of a loving mate—
To culminate,
In the fulfillment of seasonal legacy to procreate.

R A I N

Clink . . . tick . . . plop . . .

Clink . . . tick . . . plop . . .

Soft sound of droplets
Cascading down
From the gray eyes
Of a tearful sky.
An embellished cry . . . ode to a lazy lullaby,
In midst of mood-seasoned lament.
Wet-disconsolate . . .
Augment to
Warm-romantic.
Fireplace flames dance a celebration
Of difference enhanced,

Temptress, your weeping implore
No longer my soul is able to ignore.
Out of the indoor,
My enamored body is flung . . .
To among open enticement of nature
You have sung.
Fly I must, from the menagerie
      To
The drenched, the lubricated, the quenched elated
Recipient birds, animals, and flowers . . .
The ground soaked and scattered
With earth-colored Autumn leaves—
The cleansed diamond encrusted trees.

Wet-faced and exuberant,
We all cherish your watery cry . . .
Expression of seasonal love
And gift from High.

WIND

Invisible entity . . .

Puff and blow your gargantuan cheeks

Bounteous strength for incessant affair—

Wisk whimsical columns of air . . . everywhere.

Send currents of hot breath

Across the African desert

In the red dust clouds of Sirocco.

Hum tune of minstrel

Through the corridors, cracks, and crevices

Of European mountains . . . mighty Mistral.

And fan the wild fires of Southern California

With Satan Santa Ana's.

Then pause . . . to collect the accolades

Attributed to your crystal clarity.

Rarely, is there consciousness

Of your omnipresence . . .

Enigmatic span of substance nebulous.

Free spirit of capricious will . . .

Visitor of destinations incalculable.

Wonderous element,

Slipping in and out of the tangible world

To respire in Heaven and other universal environments.

FOG FACTOR

Odious odorless smoke . . .
Spread your slippery shroud of stealth;
And disperse the gray-wet blanket
Of nebulous nemesis.

Creep like the plague to blind and debilitate.
Shutdown mobility—merciless,
Obscuring and deriding to a paralysis.

   Now,

Metamorphose your murk
With refract of sunlight . . .
Paint a pastel water colored visual delight!
A backdrop for the tangible-real
And gateway to the enchanting surreal.

Mysterious, magical tease—
Elude to infinity . . .
Dispense with your indeterminable depth,
In favor of a day characterless?
The wish of a fool
Given to thought muddled or mindless!

'Tis wise to acknowledge and respect Fog's capricious devil-
deeds;
But, a mistake to degrade or extract,
A piece to life's puzzle-beautiful . . .
The diverse elemental mix
That is life bountiful.

THE TREE

Regard a tree
And see a living earthly beauty of longevity.
A spiral symphony etched in elapsed time.
Set phonograph cartridge to circular chronicle spine,
For privileged enlightenment sublime.
Superior to all secondhand archives . . .
Accounts constructed of biased eyes.
Volumes speak by the mute tree,
Ever-silent witness to recorded history.
Omnipresent observer of good, misdeed, and atrocity
Often is the time you've stood
And faced the wild-fires
That decimate your kind;
To rise in renewal of glorious germinate,
Witness to yet another Nation State.

Elevation and degradation,
You've been there . . .
Mighty ubiquitous Eucalyptus,
Nourishment for beasts of prehistoric wilderness.
And, the aristocratic Palm . . .
Conjures images of royal sultans
Or, that of The Magnificent Suleiman.
Nothing is more deeply earth rooted than is the tree.
Of these, the Giant Redwood
Is monolith to eternity,
Essence of stately majesty,
And inspirational window
To a snippet of immortality.

EXPOSE'

Envision People's minds . . . an open book

Then, have a good look.

Page after page of sordid charade . . .

Unmask the myriad of false

And opposing personas . . .

Dysfunctional-affixed runaway wheel of deception,

A steam roll down a road leading to somewhere unsavory,

And nowhere any of the attached-exposed would care to be.

Blunt reality . . .

And

Invalidity

Grip and wring your guts . . .

The unbelievable—

The inescapable truth.

Your head reels

Having to deal . . .

With The disclosure of the essence

Of your life's relations.

Caribbean Isle

Feel the beat of tropical heat . . .
Swoon to the rumble of ancient drums,
Blood-throbbing rich rum-dance of skeletons.
Immerse in night ceremony of voodoo magic,
Amid zombies and shrunken heads—
Witness to the walking dead.

Sweat-drenched natives
Stripped beyond bare necessity
In evening orgy . . .
Silent, undercurrent of despondency.
Crying plea for democracy.
Franco-Afrique Republic . . .
Replete with deplete . . .
Defoliated, denuded, dehumanized, dejected . . .
Wretched participants dancing in debility of smut, soot, dung,
And crumbling huts.

Oh, poor caribbean isle
Defiled and forsaken . . .
Without constitution to have been shaken . . .
You are HAITI . . .
Rival of hades . . .
Veritable Earth-hell . . .

The entranced,
In search of alternative place
To Earth-dwell.

SPIRIT WORLD

In the still of a dark indiscernible hour of the night,
Animals sense, and stir with fright.

Middle world unrest . . . cultural ritual test.
Other dimension dominion upheaval,
In soured mix of magic, myth, and religious evil.

Apparitions abound in heated marathon fracas . . .
The unruly spirits haunting of the heathen worthless.

Meanwhile,
The weary lie awake with rampant race of mind,
To all this, put sense
And some perspective find.

WILD DOGS OF THAILAND

Through a dark fog-shrouded haze,
A scurrilous pack of hell-hounds hunched in rage . . .
The Thai Gang Of Ten;
Under the influence of a *wild-wired* savage—
Hair electrified on end.
Their battle scarred bodies, a froth of lather and steam,
Their barred teeth, dripping a hot blood stream.
Saliva syrup-heavy suspended, dangling diseased tongues
hung from askewed hideous heads.

A score of rabid infest incisors circle around.
Eyes focal measured upon new victim found.
Lead demon lunge with a snap of powerful jaws,
A terrifying guttural growl-staccato,
Gave my heart pause.
Resigned that the killer cur knew no mercy,
I stomped the head of this evil-dread.
Onslaught initiated, there was no holding back
This ferocious canine attack!
No part of my torso did they spare—
Ripped . . . clawed—
Blood and flesh flying everywhere.
Suddenly, the carnage was lit by a bright light—
A complete retreat of night,
From a source—I know not where.
The wretched beasts vanished into thin air.
Nowhere was there a trace of this desperate affair.
I lay unscathed . . . prone on the ground.
Just to my left—
A large tooth and a puddle of blood I found.

CHINA

Grand span of land and culture
       Amid
Powerful philosophic religious order . . .
Confucianism, Buddhism, Taoism—
Contrast and transition . . .
Of Imperialist ambition.
Witness Shay, Chou, Tan, and Ming Dynasties . . .
Webbed in warlord mentality.
Constituted to individual conformity—
Creed for homogeneous civility.
Rising Sun of Genghis Khan . . .
Soiled sword—found headless dragon.
Yellow tiger of pent-up ire . . .
Giant of the East . . .
       and
Formidable beast . . .
Great walled country . . .
Protected totalitarian society.
From the West,
A suspicious eye is cast . . .
To fathom the untold mystery
That is your ultimate quest.

CELESTIAL VISITOR

Swear I saw an angel last night . . .

Bathed in light and benevolence,

Smiling a radiance that flooded

Every crevice of my bedroom's interior

With a purity of white,

That gave its wings a soft-translucent glow.

Peaceful was her presence—

Disarming and heart-throbbing . . .

Beckoning—non condescending.

Wide-eyed . . .

I reached out to touch her.

I had transgressed . . .

Crossed into dominion reserved—

She was gone!

Vanished up through the ceiling . . .

And night rushed back into the room.

FUNNEL

Prior to putting that suck-straw
To your lips,

Consider the larger taste
Of full mouth gulp and swish . . .

A parable for a life lived more fully,
Not funnel-restricted willy-nilly.

QUANDARY

Interesting . . .

The way answers

Come calling,

When least you

Expect their company.

ENCLAVE

Nurture me with diversity
Rather than shelter me
In guarded/gated communities . . .

Self-tolerant like-fellows
Smug in pseudo-safe cultural ghettos.
Characterless fabricated cities . . .
Are these boring pictures of civility—
Subdivisions of social sterility
Posed as privileged living environs . . .
Exposed as paranoid peoples encampments.

Proliferating alarmingly,
Are these inhospitable hilltop shanty towns . . .
Residents hunkered down
In deluded Nirvana found.

Nurture me with diversity
Rather than the irony
Of escape and denial,
Of human self distance,
And artificial existence.

COFFEE

A coffee culture
We are exposed to be . . .

Or maybe,

A society in thirst of conformity.

YOUTHFUL PARTY

Ice cream,

A cake,

And a Paper hat,

What ever became of that?

JUNKYARD FRIENDLY

Sat across from a junkyard sipping coffee.

Something there in that disheveled real estate

Was alarmingly familiar.

Could it be that I like messy?

Derive pleasure from disarray?

A thought most disquieting—

A thought most comforting.

DOMESTIC DUTY

Oh is it ever tiring . .

This never-ending need to house clean.

No sooner have I placed it civil,

There Is dishavel.

Evil, is this force that will not permit divorce

From incessant dusting and washing and scrubbing;

It all deserves a serious trouncing-

This exigent bouncing from environ demeaning,

To eye pleasing.

Snap my fingers . . . tweak my nose-

Hung and folded clothes.

That's the way it ought to go.

Alas, until such time,

I'm prisoner to this muddled mind.

MIS-COMMUNIQUE

A curious wanderer

Excited by explore

Of another adventure,

Cheerfully volunteered:

"I'm on my way to Bali."

A cautious entrapped

Fearful of the unknown,

Half digested the disclosure

And replied:

"What's there?"

FREE SYMPHONY

Shimmering tree bells ring
Soft . . . whispering.

Chorus wind chimes sing
Delicate . . . soothing.

A symphony of *Verde*
Hung intermittently,
Performing molto piano . . .
A peaceful soul-concerto.

Composition to human longing . . .
This, the everlasting
Rhapsody In Green.

PARADISO VISUAL

Lying in paradise,

Lapping up the happy sun . . .

Silent invasion

Of white submarine cumulus,

Spied floating high

Over a blue Bali sky.

QUIET WISDOM

Flash of teeth and eyes—

Subterfuge . . . disguise.

The wise respond,

With a slight nod of the head . . .

Curt dismissal of this dishonest dread.

FLOATING

I am floating . . .
Gently rippled in sibilant streams of liquid substance.
Crisp viscose-stimulated . . . exhilarated
Semi-submerged,
Given to glide, supple slip and slide of current . . .
Floating.

Floating am I
Airy and high
Ride upon fluff of whipped cream puffs . . .
White mounds of spiral colossus cumulus.

Sensual soar in and out of caressed
Spires and turrets . . .
Meshing and merging . . .
Wistful wind streams—
Picking up steam . . . then slowing
To relaxed meander . . .

Floating . . . floating.

PLIGHT FLIGHT

I sat in the parking lot
Under a glide path.

Airships approached,
Their bright-eye lights
Piercing the fog thickened night.

Looked up, expecting to see the ordinary;

Instead, a tri-bank of blinding lights
Gave me a fright!

Thought an Extra-terrestrial
Had brought its presence to bear . . .

A projection indelible,
Mind visited there.

QUINTESSENTIAL IRONY

She is . . .
Soft, gentile, tactile and natural.
Loved for her poise, wit, and intelligence.

She is . . .
Inexorably . . . married.

She is . . .
Hard, aggressive, truculent and painted.
Once loved for her illusion, sarcasm, and forced intellect.

She is . . .
Perennially . . . unattached.

INFORMATION MONGRELS

Loathe to encounter information pumping,
Non-rapport seeking, self-serving human degenerates!

There exists so much more
If only they ventured to open the door . . .

Instead, they choose to squint near-sighted
Through the portal's crack.

MEASURED RELEASE

We are caged wingless birds a-flight;

Bloated bodies time and space confined,

Strapped inside a "wide body" . . .

Locked in mutual constrict-struggle

To restrict the flow of exhaust-disgust . . .

The involuntary release

Of substance gaseous.

RECTAL EXAM.

Take me back to my primordial root.

> To

Explore the substance of my intestines.

> Linger there—

Lay my soul bare . . . stare . . .

Upon the vile snaking serpent of bile-disgust!

Enthralled with fibrous, essential enzyme-coated treasure trust!

> Fixated there—

Alternately crying, and elatedly weeping,

For having raw-exposed the bowel essence of my being.

ALTERED STATE

TO SIT AND CONTEMPLATE . . .

ALONE WITH YOUR THOUGHTS . . .

NO ONE OR THING DISRUPTING.

'TIS A LUXURY WE OUGHT HAVE EVERYDAY.

DO PRAY T'WILL BE THIS WAY

BEFORE HAIR AND MIND TURN THIN AND GRAY.

HAVE NO NEED TO SAY THAT LIFE HAS SLIPPED AWAY,

LEAVING A SHALLOW TOUPEE . . .

WHERE DEEP REFLECTION COULD HAVE BEEN

THE ORDER OF THE DAY.

ALTERED STATES

Ignorant . . . He was enslaved.

Informed . . . He was feared.

Confident . . . He was hated.

Liberated . . . He is indifferent!

GRANDMA'S LAMENT

"Can see just how she's made."

Express, of a Grandma distressed
With women's immodest dress.

"Where's the decency today?"

She was often overheard to say,
In utter flabbergasted, exasperated dismay.

Ophelia, has since passed away
(God rest her prudish soul)

Pray she doesn't turn in her grave
In response to my call . . .

For total clothing removal.

COMPLEMENTARY DIFFERENCES

The significance of hard, as it relates to soft,

Is best not to be underestimated.

For without the hard, where would soft be?

Probably, absent of distinction or desirability.

But alas, the hard is grossly under-rate . . .

Such is the fate of the grand if not great;

A crime, if one considers Density's qualities:

Hard is the enhancer of soft.

Hard is the antithesis of soft.

Hard is the reference and relevance for soft.

All, solid attributes beyond dispute.

Truth is . . .

Neither is of special allure

Absent the contrast in feel and texture of the other.

There is no thrill . . . where hard does not mesh with soft's will.

For all of hard and soft's intrinsic beauty . . . derived and received,

They are foremost and essentially,

Co-dependent entities.

HERMAPHRODITE

A black business suited

White Hermaphrodite

Quick-stepped into a posh restaurant . . .

Tipped her Fedora,

And set fire to cigar . . .

Alight upon golden echelon

Of eccentric persuasion—

An intriguing, enigmatic devil's advocate.

Alluring and repulsive,

Sensual and A-sexual . . .

But, on the whole

A tease sartorial.

Deep at ill-ease . . .

Compelled to do

As she damn well pleased.

HOUSE OF MIRRORS

Multiple mirrored images sting,
And the hideous Fat Lady
Is laughing . . . laughing . . . laughing . . .

Deep-throated . . . side-splitting
Mocking . . . mocking . . . mocking.

Bellow rises to a crescendo
And reflective glass shatters—
A vulnerable cranium is
Kaleidoscope Exposed . . .
Cracking . . . cracking . . . cracking.

HOMELESS HARLEQUIN

A present-day homeless he was—

Or harlequin of the past.

His clothing . . . a tattered patchwork,

His bicycle . . . floral bedecked;

A mobile bouquet whose path did intersect

That of the unicyclist.

Neither appeared the least-bit curious,

Nor did notice of the eccentricity of the other seem apparent;

As though each was encased in his private space and time
compartment—

Separate entities, possessing an invisible kinship with one
another.

The odd pair merged into the mesh of city traffic

Never to reappear;

Bizarre figures somewhat jaded,

There images swallowed up in modernity

And faded.

DESTRUCTIVE CONSTRUCTION

Construction often confounds me . . .

Man's inability to leave things be.

Flail your hammer, fell your tree—

And long for greenery.

Pave the earth's back with asphalt, concrete and steel . . .

Then look in bewilderment when in protest she

Shakes, quakes, and reels.

To hell with this compulsive need to tamper . . .

The odious primordial marking and spraying behavioral

Rancor,

Insensitive ravage of destructive construction,

And the utter waste of this sorrowful reduction.

La . . . Dee . . . Da

WHAT IS THE ULTIMATE FATE

OF

THE MOTHERSHIP PLOWING THROUGH

TIDALWAVES OF VIOLENCE?

THE QUERY BEGS THE ANALYSIS

OF

ITS MINDLESS CARGO . . .

EITHER OBLIVIOUS OR INSENSITIVE

TO THE COURSE UPON WHICH

THEIR RUDDERLESS VESSEL HAS EMBARKED.

KNOWLEDGE

I clear my mind of thought and listen.

Only then, am I able to find answers.

Knowledge, is there in nature.

A river, a bird, a rock, a tree.

Listen . . .

They shall converse with thee.

PROCREATIS OBLIVIOUS

Have another baby . . . Never mind its nurture—

Your ego will be fed.

CORRECTION OF THE RIGHT

She lies lifeless . . . prone on her death-bed.

A monitor registers a finite trace of brain activity

Emitted from her head.

Old, feeble, and unable to speak,

Her plight . . .

A distortion of a so-called "Life Right."

She is skeletal—a remnant of herself,

That is all.

Vacant eyes roll in dark hollow sockets,

Searching for mercy . . .

A deliverance from her indignity.

They implore and try to convey:

Please find another way . . .

For this, is too horrific a price to pay.

Day . . . After . . . Day . . . After . . .

UP FRONT

Say it, articulate your point . . .

Flatter—if sincere . . .

Let them know you hold them dear.

Now . . .

Voice your displeasure . . .

Real people can accept their measure.

Never bite your tongue . . .

You swallow brine and dung.

TURN ABOUT

A determined deer hunter ventured into the forest
On a dark foreboding day.
A good day thought he
To bag his quarry.
Deeper and deeper did he trek through the wilderness.
The huntsman looked up into the black sky
And decided that here! . . . was where he should try.

Patiently, the predator sat awaiting sign of his prey.
The day was rapidly growing darker
With time and condition.
He yawned and checked his ammunition.

Suddenly, a creaking and popping of twigs
He heard under hoof.
A buck of stunning beauty and grace!
The hunter and the hunted . . . face to face.
His heart leapt to his throat . . . throbbing at a furious pace.
The marksman took aim . . .
But, damn!
Just now, the weather turned nasty.

BOOM!

The buck sprang into the thick brush.
The hunter and a tree
Lay sprawled across the ground . . .

Dead.

Seems lightning was faster than
The bullet meant for the fine buck's head.

DRY FLY ANGLER

Intuition spoke . . .
And the angler's instinct listened.
The lake lay smooth as the skin of a drum-
Save for an occasional rambunctious wisp of wind
Whipping water current and Fly Fisher's
Blood-stream flow, in synchronous rhythmic ripple.

A lone Brook Trout lay in feeding lye.
Here, his casting skills he would ply.
Inspired was he, by intuitive certainty
That a big fish tread there . . . hungry

With excited respiration,
Quietly, he crept toward his rendezvous
With the mystery beneath the blue.
Ever so lightly did his fly alight upon the azure veneer.

Suddenly, a rocket burst the plane of the startled surface,
Shattering and showering
With eruptive shock and exhilarating revelation.
A thousand diamond droplets rose and fell back
Upon the point of explosion.

A gift of momentary glimpse . . .
Of multicolored beauty-
Exorcized in anguished rise.
Bent on demise of the source of its distress.

Fish and angler,
Interlocked by fine-line tether-
Combatants connected in finite struggle/pleasure.
The captured and the enraptured-
The short of breath and the breathless . . .
A dichotomy of emotional absurdity.

The angler waded hip deep to meet
His fine and powerful quarry.
Each looked upon the other . . .
The goggle-eyed awed appreciative,
And the wide-eyed anxious anticipant.

The proud fish ceased it's struggle.
The boy felt peace envelope his body.
Gently, he caressed his gallant . . .
Now languid friend,
Kissed her mouth adieu . . .
The beautiful Brook vanished into the blue.

FAULTY APPLIANCE

Someone carelessly littered the streets

With every conceivable bric-a-brac.

Just there, I noticed an electric fan running—

Wind driven . . . lying on its side . . .

Refusing to die.

THE TRIAL

A national disgrace is this O.J. Case;
Transparent, with moral and legal debase.

An open operation, in prime-time public place.
The defendant bled until dead.

Packs of whores—
Carnivores bore into the flesh of the acquitted . . .
With voracious greed jackals succeed;
Ripping and tearing the fleshy gangrene-greenbacks
from a wounded Running Back.

Knife attack . . .
Savage and cruel,
O.J., the crazed, outraged, perpetrating fool.

Given that, as a supposition of fact,
Regard the conduct of the Marauding Maggots—
Abominable, reprehensible societal acts!

      Guilty!

A society devoid of the innocent.
Realists to the farce of legal equity,
Choking on regurgitated greed.

METRONOME

Carefully, she measured her "Crack"
for a hit.

Now, she did something . . .

I could not make sense of it.

With intense scrutiny

She regarded and set

The hands of a timing device.

"My heart is too weak," she explained

"For so frequent and so heavy a dose . . .

Done as a precaution," she emphasized,

With a bob of the head

"Better this, than to be

Rendered dead.

You know,

Not too close—to prevent overdose."

"Ridiculous" was my reply

And, she commenced to get high.

With glazed eyes

She beat off the seconds

Before returning for more

Neck and head

Swaying loosely attached—time elapsed.

Disgusted with this incremental life enslaved,

Determined to never see myself that way . . .
I ran home, from this cloned Metronome.

MEDIATION

Slip into a mind-stream of quiet.

Rejoice in the absence of sound.

Return to the womb

To revel your rebirth . . .

In sensitized benefit

Of a privileged environment.

BACK TO BASICS

There once existed a time when one said what one wished to
convey.
Speaking with clarity and honesty—
Not as it is today.
Now, a subterfuge is commonly used . . .
A palate sweetened distortion of truth-abused.

Allow the offering of but a few examples of this,
The immoral twist of language amiss:

"We may have been somewhat disingenuous."
Let's not be pretentious.
A cowardly, surreptitious admission to a bold-faced lie
Is my suspicion.

"It is a process of ethnic cleansing."
It is genocide
With a nauseous, arrogant air—
The sobering essence of the barbarous affair.
It is a put-down of different . . .
An intolerance of diversity.
It is not merely mean—
It is small mindedness in the extreme.

And, what are we to make of "collateral damage"
Oh, it is something the mind can surely manage.
Several thousand dead and homeless men, women and children—
Minimize the chagrin?
If the phrase is uttered to denote an accompanying
Or supporting measure,
The price paid, is certainly an unbalanced ledger.

Let us return to some semblance of integrity.
Where statesmen perform with a degree of alacrity;
And one's intelligence is not so callously regarded.

'Tis the deceiver that is ultimately outsmarted.

With horror, one perceives an adolescent mentality run free,
Of a proportion akin to juvenile delinquency—
Children unable to state with honesty their stance,
For fear of punishment vis-a-vis rejection,
Must necessarily suffer the loss of election.

BALANCING ACT

Life . . .
That tightrope balance between
Success and strife.

The abyss awaited fallen—
The precipice greeted elevated.

Inner peace . . .

The equilibrium solution . . .
Technique for transverse-transcendence,
Of the tricky taut-walk into providential acceptance.

COMPULSION

OBSESSION WITH THINGS MATERIAL . . .

FAR FROM ETHEREAL.

ADDICTED TO POSSESS . . .

AN UNHOLY TRANSGRESS.

CEASE THIS ACTIVITY . . .

YOUR RELEASE FROM CAPTIVITY.

LIFE

So this is the essence of existence . . .

A question-marked life finite,

Influenced by an unknown omnipotent;

Devoid of compassion

For the quantum query:

Why am I here,
    and
What is the meaning of life?

Basking at the beach

My soul I did beseech.

Up from the vast sea

Emerged an explanation of profundity.

"Life, a voice counseled,

Is to be lived and enjoyed daily,

You are time diminished

With questions and analyzations repeatedly.

Live each moment as though it were your last;

In harmony with nature—to escape the morass."

Pensively, did I stop to contemplate this wisdom.

Had I lived this way, or was I micro-imprisoned;

An incarcerate constricted by mental condition,

In conflict with words so wise . . .

This revelation for conduct

Will now, my life comprise.

L I F E

The "Marathon" is short . . .

The course need not be foreshortened

With a winded spring to the finish.

EXCLAMATION

"I'm the luckiest man in the world."

A pair of lips elatedly exclaimed.

"All that matters is that you feel that way."

An overhearing pair of ears did say.

Curious, the ears queried the person

to whom the affection was directed.

"Not bad, to be so well appreciated?"

The ears offered.

"I guess so."

Was silent eye's response.

Pair of ears perked,

With detection of love abyss.

Sensing the degree to which

The relationship is at risk

For personal hurt and misery.

One, to wallow in the mud

Of the unrequited.

TRANS-MANIA

You know these ones . . .

American blondes . . .
Having their vicarious Scandinavian experiences
Strapped to a Volvo, never to venture beyond
The stimulation of their perception of the parameters
Of a conceptualized Nordic city.

The 4-wheel drive freaks . . .
Fearful of a drive over a pot-holed street.
It's the Recreational Vehicle vogue that's
Made them conformist rogues;
Represents a slight segue from the Jeep . . . It's more chic!
An utter bore, are the pony-tailed females, sporting
Their designer baseball caps.
Worse, are those perverse chaps of similar frames of mind,
sporting Schwarzenegger behinds.

And then, there's the little man in need of phallus expand.
Push'n his Porsche to the red-line, every time he "gets off"
The line . . . Severe grind of the nerves as he swerves, taking
That curve in Walter Mitty Indy. Absurdity.

We surely recall the family that buys a Mercedes Station Wagon
Purely for its beneficial safety . . . please spare me!
Status seeking in the persons of their offspring;
Not an ugly manifest, but certainly of suspect values
presentment.
Nothing wrong with the idea—
It's the surreptitious glint, that is worthy of resent.

And so must I, drive the car that is the essence of me—
I'll never divulge what the vehicle might be . . .
Think I'd knowingly expose my psyche?

COLORLESS FUN

Caution . . . yellow, color of a coward—
    Overt challenge to the tiny ego.

Stop . . . red, color of blood—
    Conjures fear and dread.

Go . . . green, non-threatening cajole—
    A false sense of flow.

      But,
Where is the benevolent light,
One that allows travel unabated?
A standard underrated!
Seems conspicuously absent
And purpose-degraded.

      Control be gone!
Enter commuter utopian.

A traffic device serving the immediate needs
Of everyone—
No more frustration . . .
Unrestricted, non-incremental, uninterrupted run—
Deregulated fun!

As for the color of this one?
Well, that's all too apparent . . .
Of course, it would be . . . transparent.

TENNIS

The perfect contest . . .

A match of will and skill—

Personal, with constant challenge to overcome.

Replete with crude riggers of war.

Battle in your *zone* . . .

The opponent's response your own.

Volley your rapier, slice your knifing serve,

Rifle that overhead—

Leave your combatant dead.

Incorporate the cerebral mix of Chess,

With Ballet-like finesse.

This, the superlative sport of Tennis.

BREATH . . . HEALTH . . . WEALTH

THROW OPEN YOUR WINDOW AND BREATHE.

REJOICE IN THE SMELL OF FRESH AIR.

REVEL IN THE GLORY OF YOUR HEALTH . . .

THEREIN LIES YOUR WEALTH.

SILENT PROTEST

Early I rise privately protesting my fate.

Gifts numerous for such an ingrate.

A groggy night peels away her dark shroud of sheets,

And the sun rises to crown a distant peek.

Chipmunks stir with dawn of light . . .

Birds sing a score of music delight.

A canopy of stars twinkle adieu,

With brilliance diminished to a gift of caribou.

Anguish be set free!

A rejuvenation overcame me . . .

I forgot to wallow in self pity.

RECOGNIZED EYES

Appalling 'tis to look into adult eyes and see
The accumulated pain and misery.
Seems universally inescapable . . .
Especially for those destined to dwell in our cities.

Perhaps, 'tis mantle for having lived—or endured
As the case may be.
Having witnessed this, It's refreshing to see a child's naivete'.

Abhorrent 'tis to identify the dead-eye suffering
In a child mired in poverty—
Theirs is overwhelming tragedy.

Fortunate are the few who've managed to evade this malaise
How wonderful to recognize youth in their gaze!

    And—

Let it be stated, that jaded/tainted mirrors of the soul,
Should be paramount of things to dread . . .
For those poor individuals are . . .

The living-dead.

A DIFFERENCE OF PERSPECTIVE

He has nothing . . . but **HE** has everything.

He sees nothing . . . but **HE** captures with vision.

He suffers . . . but **HE** enjoys

He looks outward . . . but **HE** looks inward.

He loathes loneliness . . . but **HE** finds comfort in solitude.

He passes time . . . but **HE** loves his time.

He dies . . . but **HE** lives.

CUMULUS 9th

People seeking the perfect mate—

A lonely life is often their fate.

The perfect package . . . the ideal team—

This gleam will, more often than not, lose its sheen.

For it is unrealistic—dream, what with everyone out to get

La creme de la creme.

And, this said not to faith or process demean.

Hope runneth high with all passions firmly seated

On that elusive cloud supporting our pie in the sky.

ULTERIOR

A favor given is only as good as . . .

The love bestowed with its offering.

Conditions and obligation attached . . .

The favor is detract,

Shrouded in debt that the lender

Looks to extract.

ENIGMA

Come again?

Nebulous wisp of whim.

You are strange statagem.

Sweep me up in your enigmatic fluff.

To float and fly in rose-colored sky.

Now, soar the other way, in display of depth

You've somewhere found.

Astound with constant change . . .

Perhaps, therein lies the dichotomy

That leaves me deranged.

TUBE PHILOSOPHY

"LOOK, THERE IS A WAY TO THE LIGHT!

BUT WAIT . . .

A FOOTBALL GAME'S ON THE TUBE TONIGHT."

DOING TIME

Society sits listless in a corner

Of the dark dungeon of despair . . .

Inmates of missed opportunity;

And subjects of The Magistrates edict:

A life sentence of noise and rancor,

Of incessant, omnipresent assault

To the collective senses.

This, the punishment for the

Environmentally insensitive . . .

Hell-sentenced.

Aggravated, agitated *Droids* . . .

Confined and constricted mechanisms would tight

Like clockworks in a time bomb—

Primed for implosion.

Stripped and deprived of peace and tranquillity . . .

The price paid

Is the loss of elevated creativity

And true spirituality.

LOTTO LUCKY

Why in hell can't I win the lottery?
We should all be equally unlucky.

Peacefully must I accept this disparage—
No closed-fist table pounding tantrum throw.

The result . . . the inevitable—
A resounding echo . . . No!

You did not win the lotto.

BRIGHT LIFE

Try on a smile . . .

'Twill tickle and stimulate . . .

An inner massage at cut-rate

You are of a mind to be dour . . .

Your body set to ferment and sour.

Turn upside down that debilitating frown . . .

To an early grave you are bound.

Laugh

As long,

As deep,

And as often as you can.

'Tis you see, more effective

Than the most expensive longevity tea.

Be of healthy mind and spirit . . .

The good life is elusive

We must pursue

And immerse ourselves in it.

Le MORTICIAN

A cold dark hole in the ground
Is all that one family found.

The relatives of another departed,
Discovered much to their hair-tearing chagrin,
A loved one abhorrently missing.

Yet another clan, was to suffer the hideous
Disclosure of a mind wrenching site . . .
Several bodies heaped in *helter skelter plight.*
Enmeshed flesh, and degenerated interlocked rib cages;
Most contemptuous perennial crime perpetration . . .
Throughout the ages.

Witness, the work of the scurrilous!
The proprietors of the cemetery unscrupulous.
Relievers of corps' gold fillings and jewelry stuff.
Sedentary vultures, predators without peer—
Morticians of greed and opportunity dispelled fear.

Quick to tear when relatives are near
Morbid, irreverent creatures of despicable morality . . .
Yours is a special mortality.

No need for the disembowel of your odious intestines
For your fate is inferno destined;
To burn in an eternal hell-recycled.

Penance, for all the souls
Upon which you have so grievously trampled.

SOUTHERN HOSPITALITY

Just love that southern hospitality . . .

Everything smothered in fluff and gravy.

Baby Talk

Uncomfortably bloated beach ball bubble . . .

Don't know why my soon-to-be mommy

Went to all this trouble . . .

Stretched taut-to the limit,

She's spent.

As for me, it's most unpleasant—

Claustrophobic.

Mommy's a coke addict.

Wouldn't it be wonderful

If I could talk her into . . .

Reversal.

SPACED

Poets and Jazz Artists . . .
Those departed from the docking station—
Jettisoned among the inhabitants of Constellation Creatis . . .

A billion bright stars twinkling eons of knowledge
Hung in suspension
For liberated tap, into the rarefied air
Of a special spherical dimension.

Miles, Coltraine, Dexter, Moliere, Baudelaire, Voltaire—
All have visited there.
Weighted in weightlessness . . .
Load burdened with creative compulsion—
That insatiable feminine-side Lightspeed astral ride—
Drive to the brink of mental burn up.
The stuff that provides the edge to fight complacency and rust.
So explore they must . . .
The Poets and jazz Artists, dwellers of distant galaxies,
Pupils of the pharaohs and prophesies
Possessors of special gifts . . . selectively given

By the Master Creator in heaven.

JOB RELATED

I AM . . . I EXIST . . . I KNOW,

BECAUSE I HAVE A JOB—

NO ORDINARY SLOB.

I'M AN ENTERTAINER . . .

THE WIZ OF SHOW BIZ.

AND I KNOW I AM IMPORTANT.

MY EGO TELLS ME SO.

STUPOR CLUB

Victim . . . of a down on your knees,
Heavy assault nightclub-pretentious . . .
Blasphemous enough to have assumed the name of a patron saint.

Where mimics masquerading as musicians, hide behind blaring
Audio decibels, in desperate attempt to conceal
their inadequacies;
Callously bursting delirious heads, like ripe watermelons.

It's superficial women, sport spandex skirts and pants,
To ass and vagina enhance—
Dangling their worn sexuality like sun bleached desert signs
Blowing in an arid wind.

The men . . .
Largely pathetic characters trimmed in low carat-count gold,
Slightly out of league with their gender opposed
Strip-mining sisters;

A disjointed improbably quick-mix leading to very little
Relevant substance—a journey together . . . to nowhere.

Clubbed in the dark of night,
The collective assaulted are unable or unwilling
To positively identify their assailant.

Prostrate and bleeding, your host comes to your assistance—
Insult to injury . . . smugly he runs his hands
Through the pockets of your bludgeoned body.

Where personal injury is the norm, the numbed who venture
to object,
Are fools who've found themselves stating the obvious.

So, drink up!
Joyous . . . oblivious,
And feign that all of this is non-injurious.

CINEMA PSYCHOSIS

Preen ye Kings and queens

Of the big screen;

No matter that fame is fleeting—

Your eminence largely

Of minimal meaning.

But alas,

Public adoration is Camelot—

Without which,

Regal egos rot.

EGO LINE

No wonder

Entertainers place themselves

Ego-forefront . . . sublime.

They have but to look at the poor doting fool

Who stands anticipant, at the far rear

Of their show's performance line.

QUEEEN OF THE HOP

They all gawked—

Stunned by her adornment:

An off-white, starch-stiff 50's lampshade dress,

Silver gypsy hoop earrings,

A rhinestone/garnet tiara,

And black whore's spiked heels.

She turned on them,

Departed the party—

Never uttering adieu,

Her ass fleetingly waving . . .

"Fuck you."

VIRILITY

A man of seventy, upon seeing a beautiful tree

Emoted with child-like glee.

Now there's a gentleman brimming with sensuality!

MENTAL LONGEVITY

Youth and longevity . . .

The young-aged find,

Has everything to do with

The Mind.

GARDEN DISCOVERY

Adam looked at Eve—

With each, there was an examining:

"What are those two protrusions?"

Adam asked—instinctively drawn to them.

"And your singular projection . . . rising to erection?"

Questioned Eve, excitedly.

Anatomies merged.

Answered/explored silently . . .

Exhaustively.

F l a s h

Proudly,

She drove up my drive

In a bullet-tail-lit Cadillac—

Baboon-ass pink!

FLAVOR SAVOR

A tough black lesbian

Entered an ice cream parlor;

Her demeanor saying:

"Serve me . . . don't get into my morality."

She ordered two scoops . . .

"Cheese cake" and "Divinity"—

The waitress laughed . . . good-humoredly.

The homosexual failed to see the irony.

CHILL'N

A Central Park bench

Sits at frost's perimeter

Moon misted—

Anxiously awaiting

The warm kiss

Of a sunny ass.

SERIAL SEDUCER

A serial seducer

Looked longingly at the frontal crease

Of her skin-tight pants.

Chased his would-be victim surreptitiously

Throughout the supermarket,

Only to be thwarted

By a lecherous cop—

Cuffs dangling in hand.

INDELIBLE RED

"I saw red" . . .
She was overheard to say,
As they took her away.

There was a price to pay—
Just happened to be today and this way . . .

He, with his life,
She, the haunting, recurring image of a knife.

"I saw red" . . .
Indeed she did—

The fracas forever etched
Upon her ferruled forehead.

GAME

Wish there to be sense put

To antisocial coquetry.

This irretrievable delve

Into the mucked and mired

Sham of self-deception.

A ragged rectitude reeling

From turbulent insecurity . . .

The waste, the squalor, the pity

 Let alone . . .

 Let be . . .

 These . . .

To flail in a self-fashioned

Hell-sea . . .

Of emotional poverty.

FUTURISTIC SHOPPING CART

An ear splitting sound shot from the shopping cart.

"A new invention to the homeless thwart;
When the mobile basket is taken 200 yards
From the supermart."

To this, I heatedly responded:

"Ridiculous, cold and heartless."

His retort, and conversation end:

"Only way we know to *beat the homeless my friend*."

RODEO DRIVE

I could sit here forever . . .

Never budging so much as an inch.

The permanence of beautiful female fixtures

Parading down Rodeo.

The cream of the Asians,
The alluring Italians,
The magnificent Brazilians,
The elegant Ethiopians,
The svelte Scandinavians,
And the tantalizing Californians . . .

The untouchable-unapproachable,

Each encased in her individual glamour and glory.

Each acutely aware of her attributes, flaunting them on route.

Some, natural in presentation,

Some, a self-conscious aberration.

Whatever this marvelous mix may be,

I sit here desirous of collecting each that I see,

To have and to hold for eternity—

Knowing it shall never become reality.

COQUETTE

A coy little coquette
Of a mind to toy with me,
Batted her eyes flirtatiously;
Relying upon the lady I accompanied,
To preclude my pressing her prostrate offering.

Attention seeking tease . . .
Milking her femininity
To test self-questioned desirability.

An awkward, solicitous dance . . .
The rhythm, uneven and discordant.

To Tango, my lady and I smilingly chose—
Our embrace, a virtual slap in the face.

A sand castle swept by a tide of despair,
Her granulated essence scattered everywhere . . .

Disfigured, deformed, in disarray—
Left groping for pieces of dignity,
Or perhaps, another misogynist opportunity.

SEA SIZZLE

Sizzling bursting bubble pop
Of a billion white-capped
Foamed ejaculates,

Driven from the deeps of the sea
To ride the crest—body wet.

Sperm slipping in and out
Of sea menagerie
In natural harmony—rhythmically.

Roll over one another
Again and again . . . procreating,

Sensuous splash and spray of semen
Membrane retained . . .
To impregnate . . . proliferate
In diverse resplendent gleam,
Beneficiaries of

Father Almighty's precious genes.

LOVE LIST

I love it when a powerful sea breeze
Forces fresh air into my reluctant lungs.

I love it when time is of no importance—
No schedule, and I'm unable to recall
All that I forgot I did.

I love it when machines are mute,
And my thoughts are the only disturbance.

I love it when a pretty girl is unaware of,
And non-enamored with her beauty,
And thus, shares it beautifully.

I love it when I am peaceful and able
To feel that peace in my release,
And in that of others.

I love it when everyone seems possessed
To smile the thoughts of happiness they project.

I love it when after loving,
I and my lover lie totally at rest, spent of restlessness.

I love it.

THE PLATTER

Predisposed to mind and body nurture,
To a local restaurant I ventured.

A plate setting of Italian cuisine,
With sorry seating,
Adjacent to a couple of *princesses* in the extreme.

The commence of a mindless roto-stimulus . . .
A damaged stylus, turning round worn, tired tracks of scratched
wax.

The tune, an old recycled refrain of churned, convoluted lyrics;
Surfaced, and distorted over and over again . . .

-MEN-

And the myriad of problems they present for them.

Finally had my fill—
Paid my bill, and headed for the door.

Relieved to be outside . . .
Brisk was my stride from this hideous-repetitious pair.
Oh, the smell of fresh air!

However, no sooner was I out of there,
A faint sound struck . . . boxing my ears again—

A phonograph record spin,
Stuck in regurgiation . . . grinding.

INTERACTIVE UPHEAVAL

A wholesale prevail of male versus female
Distrust has social interaction at a bust.

A simple hello, is often received with suspicion
If not outright derision.

Every conceivable scenario of eminent demise
Rises with this salutary verbal decry.

The person to whom the greeting is directed
Is certain to be derailed—put-off,
If not tied to a track.

God forbid invasive eye entrap . . .
Minds run rampant with the horrors
Of what such a truculent is attempting to extract.

The fervor . . . the guile!
To be targeted to reciprocate a smile.
"Give an inch, take a mile"

While all of this is abhorrent,
The cardinal sin, is to touch . . .
Carnal implications run amuck.
A serial rapist!. . . .
It's you he's out to fuck.

Why not cloak ourselves in the feign
Of holiday cheer . . .
Temporarily erase the fear;
Conveniently pretend we're not
Paranoid Puritans.

Sort it out in our heads . . .
Perhaps, cordial interaction on our streets,
Won't run-up the red flag in our beds.

SUFFERING STRANGER

Met a lady severly injured
By inordinate strife.

With difficulty, she recounted
Her calamities:

First a husband, then a niece—
Dead within a few weeks . . .
Victims of separate air disasters,
And of dubious official closures.

One time wife, mother eight . . .
With God she entrusts *her fate.*

With far away expression,
She confesses her depression . . .

Spends enormous time and money
Doing alone, the things together,
They had promised . . . postponed.

Curiously,
Our meeting place was the exterior of
The Haunted House of Disney.

Upon her emergence from the ghostly structure,
She tearfully needed to utter this disclosure:

"It's only a solo fulfillment of our dreams;
But in some small way, it revitalizes the duality . . . Sorry.

A confidant, she sorely needed.
She proceeded to tell that which preceded.

MAN AND MOUSE

A man crossed the street
At 4th and Main.

Huddled in a blanket,
The sensitive could see
The struggle to maintain dignity.

The faded comforter sported washed-out
Inanimate images of Mickey.

Ironic to see a grown man
Down and out . . .
Parading about,
Cradled in the likeness
Of America's favored
Commercial Mouse.

THE RECKONING

Temple walls vibrate faith,
Exciting astral minds to levitate;
Ascending high, to a billion rings of halo-aglow.

The faithful smile,
Anticipant of sacrament and halogen anointment.

Disappointment!

A powerful magnetic force
Pulls the worship majority around,
To accept the *other dominion's thorny crown.*

LISTEN

Speak to me . . .
You mute/inanimate rock or tree.
Tell me how humankind
Has left nature bereft.

Share your sorrow for my kind—
Blind to the essence of our joint existence.

Open up—expose the quandary.
Tis, a small favor for empathetic inhabitant
In search of Planet Savior.
Disturbed behavior—
A challenge to the end . . .
Earth brought to brink—pushed to fend.

Confide my friends, and God speed.
Your tale of tales, to make ears bleed!

DELUSION

Reprehensible is the carnival flaunt

Of physical features-illusional;

A base-instinct circus arousal:

The freak, the clown, the slight of hand . . .

The charlatan—

Parading distort-painted,

In slick-trick tainted allure . . .

Far from demure.

You are the quintessential bore . . .

The garishly accentuated-compromised insecure.

DEPRECIATED CURRENCY

Money have you to exclude and isolate . . .

The price you've paid

Is far greater

Than a loving self can appreciate.

DOGGED

Wrenching to see
A black Lab puppy tied to a tree . . .
Brow beat—admonished mercilessly;
Hands crashing across the dog's defeated face,
Made me want his master
To suffer the pain of similar disgrace.

In show of remorse,
The master sought shared solace,
Stroking the spirit-wounded
With guilt-ridden pace.

Hideous to see demented animals
Emanating misery in duality.

Man . . .
Pitifully power concept sick,

His "best friend" . . .
The beleaguered neurotic—

Companions . . .
Choke-chained, life drained—
Strangle-stranded from peace . . .
Entities tethered to an agitated leash.

CONFORMITY

Thought about conformity
And how utterly debilitating
Is this cancerous deformity . . .

Collapsed bodies . . . innards eaten—
Devoured by insidious acquiescence;
Suffocating, contorted
Gut twisting squeeze . . .
Deteriorating to
A hemorrhagic finality bleed;

Death by assent—
Terminal breath-draw of constricted individuality,
Spent to a sibilant last gasp.

Submission . . . capitulation!

NO!

Venture brazen . . .
Beyond contrived horizons—
To a healthy condition . . .
Mind and body in harmonious-synchronous soar . . .
A rewarding self-fashioned personal explore.

THE WAGER

Run thoroughbred—
Red-hot equine . . .
Mad dash for the finish line.
Midget-man flailing whip in hand . . .
Extend to exhaustion—

Revenue riding your high-strung head,
Prove yourself a bundle of funds—
The gallant one,

Run . . . run . . . run . . .
Throw no caution to the **win** . . .
Destined perennial loser . . .
Indentured . . . wagered . . . spent—
To the last **red** cent.

MOON RENDEZVOUS

A flush amorous Moon
Captured me . . .
Gravity retrieved into it's galaxy.

Moving into proximity,
I detected a magnificently crevassed forest,
Undulating in a slow pulsating orbital rotation—
Irresistible sensual presentation.

An alluring sphere, imploring me to abandon chaste reserve . . .
To plunge into her circular curve.

Passionately, I seized this galactic body,
Initiating the probe—
Black Hole vacuum swallowed . . .
Pressed into rarified atmosphere;

A kaleidoscope of studded stars
Imploded and exploded
In response jubilant!

The Moon slowed it's circular rotation,
Gradually **came** in delirious, spent culmination.

We lay in Celestial disorientation—
Dazzled-dazed in cosmic space;
Ecstatic with the consummation
Of a joined **asstral** ride . . .
Two hot heavenly bodies
In stimulus collide.

CREDO

I am she . . .
And she me . . .

Indubitably separate entities
Intertwined by love
And mesh of minds.

Times we find
Thoughts overlap in stimulus
Process capture—

A validation of our love enrapture.

This, the essence of compatibility—
Certainly not devoid of difficulties . . .

But, a mutual desirability we see,
And tacitly agree
To be all that personal evolution
Compels us to be.

TRANSITIONS

Allow my life the exchange
Of seasonal change,
So that I am acutely aware
That I exist;
As one comes
And another exits.

The death of autumn's leaves
Arrives with regularity—
So, is this occurrence
A certainity for all humanity.

The emergence of spring's
Birth anew—
Morning blanket of dew
Rest upon the hills
Of fresh green hue . . .
Ushering animal offspring due.

Correlated/interrelated—
One to the other . . .
Soft and distinct—
There . . .
Blowing in transitory air;
Coloring me with glee,
Feeling relationship with
The transience of every living thing;

Exhilarate—brushed in broad strokes
Of life's grand transformation.

SACRAMENT

The newlyweds exited the chapel;
Bride gushing tears . . .
Cupping her bleeding ears.

Joy of marriage?. . .
Quite the contrary;

Devastation mainfest,
Of the groom's whispered disparage.

"Frankly, I don't give a damn about love."
He callously disclosed.

"Then why in hell did you say . . .'I do'—
May I ask *this* of you?"

"Certainly,"
Was the cad's reply—
Said with a rue look in his eyes.

"You see my darling,
I am a most selfish person—
As are you . . .
Look deep into your fibre—
It's indisputably true.

Honesty, is the vow upon which our relationship shall flourish.
It is not a love for you my heart feels . . .
It is love for the feeling my heart has when I'm with you."

"Only now do I understand this feeling we both command.
With the strength of this wisdom, our marriage will forever stand."

"Amen my love,
Amen."

DIVINE DIVIDE

It was a day that none there can now remember;
An event so abjectly wrenching,
One's brain refused memory etching—
Mercifully shutting down
With pain overload . . . drown.

And conversely,
A heretofore unknown ecstasy
Never fathomed before—
Locking the mind into a befuddled box drawer . . .
A compartment absent the tools of articulation.

Only a vague haze lingered over the event—
Save for a nebulous presentment,
All details . . . curiously absent.

Both sets of Subjects,
Witness to the day the sky parted . . .
Each to experience a personal examination
Of his or her constitution;

A confrontation with the omnipotent . . .
Man prostrate, vulnerable . . . sacrificial,
Object of the ultimate observation.

A base bowel wrench—
The stench of a billion Earth inhabitants
Raw-exposed . . . guts laid open
Spewing hemorrhagic excrement—
Swimming in pools of vile bile—
Steam rising from hot decomposing innards,
To form a huge odious sulfur cloud
Above the ruin of their heaped carcasses.

While aerated others floated flush—
Rapturous in unimaginable subliminal loft.
Haloed, glowing entities . . .
Peaceful amid environmental calamity.

Acclamation
Exaltation
Purification
Validation
Benediction . . .
Bestowed upon the body of Man

In accord with The Master's Plan.

Imprecation
Dejection
Putrefaction
Invalidation
Malediction . . .
Maggots' infest of those individuals
Run afoul of the omnipotent's judgement.

This,
The day the sky gaped open . . .
A benevolent invitation to unification;
Preview of the irreversible.

The next arrival many be the final call—
Come that one,
No one will suffer loss of memory recall;
An impact eternal,
Upon living creatures . . . et al.

REBELLION

I absorbed the substance of dusk;
Devoured it's amenities . . .
Stuffed myself with feast.
Then, sat satiated . . . sedated, peaceful and serene . . .
And drank in the following:

The deep-blue sleepy celestial
Sparkle-splash of diamonds,
Expanding in size and value;
In concert with the darkening sky's hue.

Juxtaposed,
A meandering sentinel of forest green silhouetted trees,
Standing in grand relief against a fleeting metamorphosed
backdrop;
Stalwart, solid, quiet strength, ever there—
Fibrous, firmly rooted tangible fare.

Cool sprinkler soaked grass lawns
Lying in fresh-cut repose,
Emitting a soothing fragrance . . .
Euphoria for this pollution exposed nose.

An embellishment of old fashioned languid torch lamps,
Highlighting a cloudy mist left hovering over the cobbled road;
Carrying delighted eyes off into infinity.

HADES!

True life foiled by the infernal artificial;
One or a myriad of man's monstrous machines . . .
Grinding, attacking, assaulting the senses . . .
Excruciating, debilitating cut to the bone—
Won't leave me alone . . .

Nagging, gnawing pesky blood sucking gnats—
Ever a threat; returning again and again . . .
Agonizing dark cloud in the air—
Pain in the derriere!

Wrenching me from peace—
Taking me somewhere unsavory,
Draining life to a listless acquiescence of depletion and poverty.

HURRAH!

The damn alarms, sirens, street blowers, helicopters and chopper
cycles
Have gone . . . moved on—to meanace other environs.
But they will come again—return with dread . . . of this I'm
certain.

Relentless is this scourge . . . odious out of touch ruckus!
Pressing beyond civility—all manner of decency:
Cheated.
Disrupted.
Desensitized.
Corrupted.

Relinquish a measure of relief:

To think.
To thank.
To create.
To contemplate.

Grant us the sensibility and ability,
To seek and savor a space
Removed from the manufactured manure—

A madness retreat . . .
Deplete of the unnerving grind and chatter—
Devoid of the senseless inhumane mechanical matter.

Oh, to rock in my lawn chair—
No fear of noise disrupt,
Under the spell of evening's crisp refreshing air—
Escape to that idyllic island mental pictured . . .

A relic of reality.

If life's quality continues incessantly impaired,
Perhaps **rebellion** is what's needed
To have sanity mercifully spared.

LOVE INTERACTIVE

Morning's proud cock crows boastful . . .

Midday's Languid love dove stimulates coo echo . . .

Midnight's pussycat screams ecstatic approval of tomcat beau.

—COITUS INTERRUPTUS—

As love penetrates their window

THE AGE OF DISCONTENT

Once again this disturbing dream grips me . . .
A large skeletal hand reaching into my intestines,
Wringing it irrevocably dry of content;
Space and time locked within . . .
The Age of Discontent

Hollow souls transport
Deep sunk eyes;
Sockets lock-stepped
In discordant unison.

No one dare look upon the other;
Each brushed past,
In fear of the consequence of interactive introspection .
A superimposed mirrored image of Lucifer,
Trapped in the collective eyes of passers by—
Fragments of self-recognized human flesh and bones
Dangling an over-sized, hideously askew scarlet mouth.

The dregs . . .
The intellectual brain dead,
flounder in an inextricable quagmire of shallowness;

Chaotic bodies at odds with themselves reflect . . .
The coloring book of the regressed infant;
Pierced flesh, statement of the discontent;
Florescent hair, symbol of abject despair.

Malcontents everywhere . . .
Walking monuments to societal decadence;
In desperate bid for escape to relevance.

But, the oppositive is omnipresent—
A self-clone springs up on every other street corner
Mocking the absurdity of free entity.

Better that this be a bad dream
Rather than an horrific reality . . .
Somebody please wake me!

PRIMA DONNA JONES

An old tarnished star of the cinema screen
Recouped her audience with a tantrum-scream . . .
Siren for a misplaced pair of precious earrings.

Castigations followed recriminations, followed accusations;
A litany of suspicion and derision, crowned with a curse
For those averse, to this tirade gone perverse.

Pacing and placing the value of the lost jewelry's worth,
The distraught starlet drew tight,
The strings of her mental purse.

Enter the mind bend:

Like a fat hen,
Her over-sized ass was found hatching the gems!

Bloodied by the claws of her own tomfoolery,
The poor heroine was never seen again—
Pecked her way off . . . to diamond-caged oblivion.

THE MEETING
and the
REGULATORY BEAM

A luminous red standard separated us . . .
Passion partitioned by artificial beam
And asphalt abyss—tried our patience;

An unnatural impediment . . .
Akin to a nanny assigned the elderly—
But we were two vigorous energies . . .
Primed, juice-pumped—anticipant.

The discordant . . .
A stagnant sentinel-retard of spontaneous,
Sign posted imposition . . . a moment for reflect;
What more should one expect?

An inordinate eternity elapsed . . .
Finally . . . green!

We met in the center of the abyss and rushed a kiss.
A fraction of a second saw us running for our lives—
It was red—and full throttle ahead.

SPELLBOUND

Witchcraft has my phallus crave-attract
To a wild sorcerized apex;

Powerless to resist the wet palpitating kiss
Of mesmerizing membrane orifice.

Mind straight jacketed to pubis convergence—
Conjurer possessed—obsessed with carnal chant enchant.

Exuberant soar of breathless vigor—afire for more . . .
Intoxicate-flushed . . . a romp-zealous,
Succumb amid a wicked-hot lubricious abode.

Essence entranced . . . Nirvana found,
In spellbound rapturous round.

CYNIC WISH

My fervent wish is . . .

To rid my life the lips of

Disingenuous Bitches;

Those despicable Damsels

Dripping honey dipped morsels

Of masticated Penis!

TELL-TALE LIPS

Odious is the express

Of distaste for women

Confided by gents

Saddled with the lingering scent

Of a thousand pussies riding their lips.

MOUNT LASCIVIOUS

Boy, is this nifty . . .
Me, slip-sliding
In semen starch-sticky

Wow, a most sublime condition
Fantasy flight found fruition-
In cupped hand, peak-forested

A monument monolith hot-melted,
Quivered-erupted!

Now, a transformation of character . . .
Minute, mute-irresolute;
Shrivel, shrunk-cute.

And deliriously peaceful to boot!

—FLESH OBSESSED INTOXICANTS—

Sat in the psychotic sector
Of a bar bulging with lunatic intoxicants.
Battling sickness in my stomach,
And a head-reeling hangover from visual depressants . . .
Dizzied by the incessant circling and sniffing of
Sexual apparatus, by the *strange flesh* seeking obsessed;
Searching to suck the least of the soured fluids,
From an array of provocatively dressed carcasses.

Orifices drip anticipant—
The gender differed . . .
Pumped hard,
Or deflated limp—
Cursing impotence.

A primal ritual . . .
Plunged into the deeps of perversion
Of alcohol persuasion.

Basic meat . . .
Raw soft tissue, and bone-in gristle—
Fantasy merge—hot converge
In a well of beers, martinis and cognac—
Maniacs mind set to mate and copulate.

Later for the prophylactic . . .
Stimulus-plus, is the name of this thrust!

It's just the wonderful memories
Associated with this meaningful stuff,
That has them in a rut;
Now faced with the light,
Of a new dark truth—

HIV . . . POSITIVE PROOF!

VICTORIA

She flew into my space
From an electrifying place;
Flitted here and there
Soul sprinkling spirited air.

Young and fair—
Chestnut hair—
A new chapeau . . .
Crown apropos,
　—and—
Cloak of masked fragility.

One dark day,
Her bonnet whisked away . . .
Barren!
Slave to vile relentless wind;
A sickening sibilant sting—
Deafening sirens . . .
Assaulting impressionable ears.

Now, nothing remained akin
To the life that once lived within—
A ghost vanished to antiquity—
A triumphant victory . . .
A will killed—
Victim to the company of misery.

Deep circles run around
Sockets of her constitution—
The malnutrition of a man's volition.

The warm, vibrant—
Turned bleached blonde—
Blanched, sallow soul—
Paled . . . impaled sorrowful woe . . .

Stake driven deep-purposeful control.

A tiny glimmer of hope . . .
The other day, her hands
Seemed to have slipped between
The suffocating noose rope—
The dark stangle-hold left to grope.

This story continues to unfold . . .
The ending unforetold.

An optimist bets she will overcome
Her oppressor's sought conquest;

Odds makers say
She will suffer a slow,
Potential-wilted death.

The compassionate, take cheer
In the vitality of the human spirit;
Against all evil . . .
Will not quit!

PLASTIC PROVOCATION

Discerning I certainly have become . . .
And more than begun to see the scum,
Curdled sour beneath the powered/perfumed
Surface of so many women;

Sorted, superficial, artificial-sweet samplers
Shaped, contoured, and conformed,
To the constricts of fashion trends,
Swirled in a perverse griping wind-
Wispering the vulgar obscene.

The leotard loin apex ruse—
A vagina accentuated noose—
Duped penis cajole obsessed of crevess—
Roped, wrung, hung deflate-induced;

Sleeze gorilla tease . . .
Red ribbon wound, passed up
That raw-pink baboon ass,
Brought neatly around the neck,
Tied into a pretty bow—
Sign post packaged from head to toe.
Bundled for plunder—
Torts protect tarts from anarchy,
Saving rambunctious panties from rip asunder.

Cut an eye of disaproval and indignation
As uninvited eyes have you violated—
Provocation comes to a head—
Exercise the right to be selective,
It's for you to chose the primate you bed!

So, go ahead . . .
Press your pliant plastic
Up against the hard metal body

Of your knight in shining armor;
Fighting for the improbable mesh
Of dissimilar substance;
Screaming out for relevance.

An unaffected natural woman,
Devoid of insecurities and conceit—
This, all men long to meet;
Tiring of the slithering-sliding serpents
That are the usual unwholesome wholesale meat.

THE AMAZON

A black guillotine blade
Falls heavily from a twilight
Amazonian sky—
A swift barbarous cut to darkness;
Decimation and death.

Corps of a Rain Forest
Lay hacked hemorrhagic;
The great body uttering
A gasping plead for mercy,

The collective indigenous cringe with empathy,
As another wave of death-encrust razors
Ravish tropical foliage,
Rendering animal life to a desperate forage.
Everywhere is heard the ear piercing scream
Of laid waste carnage.

Anticarcinogen . . .
Every conceivable form of medicine—
Never to be—
Destined to inferno, cut from the graces
Of civilization's infirmaries;
Short sided greed . . . monumental misdeed—
A perpetration of incalculable gravity for all humanity.

And end to this insanity!
Man . . . removed from nature,
Reliant upon a brain that exercises intelligence,
Fast-destined to extinct creature;
Victim of ignorance,
And the reckless run of his hands!

Given an opportunity for an eleventh-hour reprieve—
Vis-a-vis the emergence of an enlightened generation,
Possibly there will exist a wondrous region
Known as the Amazon.
Opportunity missed—
One may readily envision,
A foreseeable end to civilization.

About the Author

Stanton Kelley is a native of Los Angeles currently living in Santa Monica, California. He studied Humanities at The University of California in Los Angeles. Stanton is also a former student of life and it's teachings, as well as a keen observer of people and the human condition. He has a son, Keith, and five goldfish. The author is an avid outdoors man and enjoys fly fishing, tennis, jogging, and skiing.

Other works by Stanton Kelley: *Memories Masculines*, a novel that has received accolades and book cover endorsement from John Gray, Ph.D., best selling author of *Men are From Mars, Women are From Venus*.